THE IRAQI FAMILY COOKBOOK

THE HIPPOCRENE COOKBOOK LIBRARY

Afghan Food & Cookery
Alps, Cuisines of the
Aprovecho: A Mexican-American Border
   Cookbook
Argentina Cooks!, Exp. Ed.
Belarusian Cookbook, The
Bolivian Kitchen, My Mother's
Brazil: A Culinary Journey
Cajun Cuisine, Stir the Pot: The History of
Calabria, Cucina di
Chile, Tasting
China's Fujian Province, Cooking from
Colombian Cooking, Secrets of
Corsican Cuisine
Croatian Cooking, Best of, Exp. Ed.
Czech Cooking, Best of, Exp. Ed.
Danish Cooking and Baking Traditions
Danube, All Along The, Exp. Ed.
Emilia-Romagna, The Cooking of
Egyptian Cuisine and Culture, Nile Style:
English Country Kitchen, The
Estonian Tastes and Traditions
Filipino Food, Fine
Finnish Cooking, Best of
Germany, Spoonfuls of
Greek Cooking, Regional
Haiti, Taste of
Havana Cookbook, Old (Bilingual)
Hungarian Cookbook, Exp. Ed.
India, A Culinary Journey
India, Flavorful
Iraqi Family Cookbook
Jewish-Iraqi Cuisine, Mama Nazima's
Kerala Kitchen, The
Laotian Cooking, Simple
Lebanese Cookbook, The
Ligurian Kitchen, A
Lithuanian Cooking, Art of

Malaysia, Flavors of
Middle Eastern Kitchen, The
Naples, My Love for
Nepal, Taste of
New Hampshire: from Farm to Kitchen
New Jersey Cookbook, Farms and Foods of
   the Garden State:
Ohio, Farms and Foods of
Persian Cooking, Art of
Pied Noir Cookbook: French Sephardic
   Cuisine
Piemontese, Cucina: Cooking from Italy's
   Piedmont
Polish Cooking, Best of, Exp. Ed.
Polish Country Kitchen Cookbook, The
Polish Heritage Cookery, Ill. Ed.
Polish Holiday Cookery
Polish Traditions, Old
Portuguese Encounters, Cuisines of
Punjab, Menus and Memories from
Romania, Taste of
Russian Cooking, The Best of
Scottish-Irish Pub and Hearth Cookbook
Sicilian Feasts
Slovenia, Flavors o
South Indian Cooking, Healthy
Spain, La Buena Mesa: The Regional
   Cooking of
Sri Lankan Home Cooking, Rice & Curry
Trinidad and Tobago, Sweet Hands: Island
   Cooking from
Turkish Cuisine, Taste of
Tuscan Kitchen, Tastes from a
Ukrainian Cookbook, The New
Ukrainian Cuisine, Best of, Exp. Ed.
Warsaw Cookbook, Old

THE IRAQI FAMILY COOKBOOK

KAY KARIM

Hippocrene Books, Inc.
New York

For information, address:
HIPPOCRENE BOOKS, INC.
171 Madison Avenue
New York, NY 10016
www.hippocrenebooks.com

   Library of Congress Cataloging-in-Publication Data
Karim, Kay.
 The Iraqi family cookbook / Kay Karim.
     p. cm.
 Includes bibliographical references and index.
 ISBN 978-0-7818-1288-7 (pbk.)
 ISBN 0-7818-1288-7 (pbk.)
 1. Cooking, Iraqi. 2. Cookbooks. I. Title.
 TX725.I72K37 2012
 641.59567--dc23
                                                  2012003357

Printed in the United States of America.

*I dedicate this book to the loving memory of
my mother, aunts, and grandmother,
who had a very big influence on my life.*

CONTENTS

ACKNOWLEDGMENTS

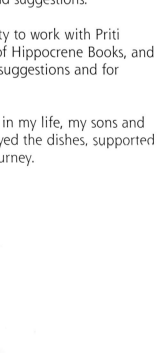

I offer my sincere thanks to my sister Samar, who emailed me many of her dessert recipes, shared her old wine recipes, and reviewed all the recipes in the book to make sure they are authentic.

Many thanks to my sister Maysoon, who spent hours in the kitchen preparing the appetizers and fish dishes.

I am indebted to culinary historian Dianne King, who took a serious interest in the Iraqi cuisine, for her suggestions and encouragement.

I am also grateful to Jacquelyn Brady, my friend and editor, who helped me throughout the writing of the chapters of this book.

I offer my heartfelt thanks to my excellent designer Alla Vysokolova for a few of her photographs.

Thanks to my brilliant editors Sheilah Kaufman and Paula Jacobson for their wonderful work and suggestions.

I am so lucky to have the opportunity to work with Priti Chitnis Gress, the Editorial Director of Hippocrene Books, and want to thank her for her insightful suggestions and for allowing my voice to shine through.

And a final thank you to the people in my life, my sons and friends, who always tasted and enjoyed the dishes, supported me, and advised me through this journey.

AUTHOR'S PREFACE

When I was a young child in Iraq, foods tasted so much better since they were organically grown. I was lucky enough to enjoy locally farmed, seasonable vegetables at practically every meal. Even now as an adult in the U.S., my weekly visits to the farmers market always bring the fresh tastes of my childhood rushing back to my mind. I like to provide my family with something akin to the tastes, flavors, and quality of the seasonal vegetables I enjoyed as a child, and you can do the same for yours.

Since the general public in the U.S. does not have any idea about Iraq's cuisine and customs, my purpose in writing this book is to introduce the Iraqi cuisine to its readers so that they can appreciate the variety, simplicity, and flavors of Iraqi dishes. The recipes that I included in this book are what my mother and sisters cooked and what I grew up eating. My mother was our role model in the kitchen at home. She was a professional teacher and a dedicated mother. Our days would start with she and my grandmother preparing a full breakfast for us every morning consisting of soft-boiled eggs, jam, cream, cheese, and tea with milk. At the same time, my mother started preparing the lunch meal by partially cooking the meat so that when she got home after school and my father arrived home we could all sit around the table and enjoy the big lunch meal of the day around 2pm. Then we rolled out the mats and took an afternoon nap until 4 pm. After that we prepared tea and served light snacks of cheese and *klecha* cookies.

Growing up in Iraq, my sisters and I cheerfully took on the traditional female roles of kitchen helpers as we assisted my mother, grandmother, or aunt in preparing the big meal of the day. Some of my fondest memories are of sitting around the kitchen table enjoying this big meal. After the meal, my sisters and I were assigned the job of washing the dishes, cleaning the counters, and mopping the tiled kitchen floor daily with warm soapy water. I come from a large family of great cooks and big eaters. My mother and her sisters were the master chefs who taught us that food is love, and it is a very important part of our family relations and hospitality. We always had our doors open for relatives, neighbors, and guests who dropped in and stayed for dinner. (When I got married, came to the United States, and started working full time, my husband always surprised me with guests he had invited for dinner to our house. When I returned home from work, I went directly to the kitchen to unwind and create some appetizing dishes. I learned early on how to get organized by preparing meals and appetizers and freezing them which came in handy when we had these unexpected guests.)

During the holidays in Iraq, we spent days in the kitchen helping out with the desserts and the main meal. The typical custom was for all relatives to pay a visit to the home of the oldest son in the family for lunch or dinner. When neighbors visited to give us their holiday greetings, they were hosted with *klecha*, holiday cookies, tea, coffee, and candies.

Even when we were very young children, we all helped in the kitchen. We peeled vegetables, cut green beans, cracked the walnuts to make holiday cookies, and brushed the cookies with the egg wash before baking. During the summer, everybody helped to make tomato paste. It was a very long process of crushing the soft tomatoes, straining the juice, and pouring it into large circular trays twenty inches in diameter. These trays were placed under the burning summer sun to evaporate the juice. We would stir the tomatoes a few times a day and in less than a week we had a supply of tomato paste for the whole year. Tomato paste is a key ingredient in most Iraqi vegetable and meat stews. Fresh tomatoes are very rare during winter, therefore families prepare these seasonal produce for later use by freezing or canning. Many families purchase a commercially produced tomato paste to supplement their needs.

My father used to go to the market and bring home the seasonal vegetables, like okra, to prepare for winter. We cut the stems off and strung them with a cord to hang on a line or in the pantry to dry. Pickling was another big family affair. We used to get bushels of cucumbers, small eggplants, and green peppers and pickle them in big pottery jars to last us a few months. These pickles accompanied every meal and were also added to salads.

During the winter, we would buy boxes of oranges and lemons to make lemon juice and orange drink (*sharbat*). We also made seasonal jams. During the winter, we made pomelo and marmalade jams, and we would eat the apricot, plum, fig, and other fruit jams that we had prepared during the summer. Fresh grapes, peaches, plums, and other fruits are not available in the market during winter so dried fruits and nuts are consumed after meals during winter. These fruits and nuts are transported from Mosul and Kurdistan to Baghdad and the other cities. We used to buy long strands of dried figs. Villagers in the northern part of Iraq harvest the figs, dry them, and string them in a long thick string and hang them in the candy and nut shops. We used to buy a few kilos of dried raisins, a variety of dates, walnuts, almonds, pistachios, dried apricots, and a mixture of seeds like pumpkin seeds and watermelon seeds. And we snacked on them while sitting around the kerosene heater in the living room during cold winter nights. We did not have central heating, but we had a kerosene or a gas heater in every room in the house.

I carried the traditions of my Iraqi childhood with me when I came to the United States and made sure that my family here enjoyed the same flavors and dishes I grew up with. My sons are now grown, but they remember when they were young, spending their time surfing in the waters off Virginia Beach and walking home with their friends to my kitchen to have a snack before returning to the beach. I spent the summer in the kitchen cooking and preparing cakes, pastries, and big meals for them. I've always felt that when you cook for someone, you are providing love. My sons always remember these happy times growing up.

In this cookbook, I simplified my cooking processes to save time and energy, and most meals made with these recipes can be prepared in less than one hour. The more elaborate meals, such as *kibbi* and *dolma*, can be reserved for the weekends. I also used easily found supermarket ingredients to prepare these authentic, traditional recipes, and photographed them in my own kitchen. All ingredients and recipes in this book have been tested to make sure the outcome is successful.

I suggest you read the spices chapter before starting to cook the recipes in this book. There I provide the ingredients for the Arabian Spice (*Bahar*, page 22) that is commonly used in Iraqi dishes, much like black pepper is used in Western dishes.

It is my pleasure to share these memories and recipes from my family with you. I hope you will in turn enjoy them with your families and friends for years to come.

Kay Karim

MOTHER'S GARDEN

My childhood home was surrounded by a garden. My father was a teacher, an artist, and a master gardener. He surrounded himself with colors and you could always find him in the garden watering and caring for the flowers, fruit trees, and herbs. People in Iraq take a great deal of pride in their gardens, since they use them to entertain their guests during the summer. When the sun went down we spent late afternoons and evenings in the garden as it was a cool place to be during the summer. When my father passed away, my mother enlisted the aid of the gardener who cared for all the gardens in the neighborhood, and was able to carry on my father's tradition.

The gardener planted a variety of flowers: zinnias, snapdragons, dahlias, and other seasonal flowers in the front yard. The garden was enclosed by a high brick wall to provide privacy. We entered the garden through the front gate to the driveway, which was covered with a grapevine trellis. It was a standard practice to plant grapevines in the garden, not so much for the grapes but for the leaves. Therefore, we planted green grapes and light red grapes that produced the right leaves for the *dolma* dish. We collected these leaves, and Mother made nice big stacks of them and put them in a plastic bag in the freezer for use during the winter. Sometimes she rolled stacks of fresh grape leaves and put them in pickling jars and poured salt water over them and sealed them.

Fruit trees surrounded the garden walls. We had citrus, apple, pear, pomegranate, fig, and apricot trees. We made seasonal jams and enjoyed the fresh fruit for

snacks. The garden also had patches of fragrant roses that my mother used to pick to make rose petal jam.

In the spring, the garden was filled with the fragrance of the citrus fruit buds, which we collected and dried. We put them in small cloth bags and hung them in the closets to freshen our clothes. Mother made orange *sharbat* during the winter. We used to spend hours in the kitchen squeezing the oranges to extract their juice. Mother added a lot of sugar and put the juice and sugar in a big pot on low heat to dissolve the sugar and make a syrup. When cooled, she poured it in bottles and sealed the cork with wax. The pantry shelf was filled with bottles of different flavors of *sharbat* to serve our guests during the summer.

The backyard had a large olive tree that produced big green olives. Mother assigned us the job of collecting these olives and pounding each olive with a stone or using a knife to make a few slits in each olive. We dropped these olives into a pail of water. Every day, my grandmother would pour the water out and refill the pail of olives with fresh water to remove the bitter flavor of the olives. This process took a few weeks. Then the olives were ready to pickle with water and salt brine and sometimes vinegar.

We also had patches of herbs and vegetables in the backyard. Mint grew wild, but we planted parsley, radishes, okra, green beans, and tomatoes. We used natural animal fertilizer instead of chemicals to fertilize the bushes.

My mother loved her garden. As soon as she got up in the morning, she prepared her breakfast, put it on a tray, and carried it outside where she sat to enjoy her garden. She watered the plants every morning and late afternoon since we had very hot summers. When the sun went down, we took out the folding chairs and arranged them in the front yard to wait for visitors and neighbors to drop by for

tea or coffee and to catch up with the neighborhood gossip. I carried my mother's tradition with me when I came to the U.S. I always take my morning cup of coffee and sit in the backyard to enjoy the flowers and feed the wild birds.

My mother in her garden with my son, 1995

IMPORTANT DATES IN THE HISTORY OF IRAQ

10000 B.C.	Mesopotamian culture is born.
4000–2350 B.C	Sumerians live in Mesopotamia and develop the cuneiform writing system.
2350 B.C.	Sargon establishes the Akkadian Empire that extends from Syria to the Arabian Gulf.
1894–1594 B.C.	Babylonian Dynasty is ruled by eleven kings over 300 years.
1792–1750 B.C.	Hammurabi becomes king of Babylon and unites the warring states.
1600–609 B.C.	The Assyrians control Babylon.
858–627 B.C.	Nineveh is the oldest and most populated city of Ancient Assyria. It is located on the east bank of the Tigris River opposite the modern city of Mosul.
605 B.C.	King Nebuchadnezzar II rules Mesopotamia and builds Babylon. Babylon's Hanging Gardens are considered one of the seven wonders of the ancient world.
539 B.C.	King Cyrus of Persia gains control of Mesopotamia and annexes Iraq. Babylon becomes the richest Persian province.
331 B.C.	Alexander the Great conquers Mesopotamia. Babylon becomes the leading city and cultural center.
141–129 B. C.	Other foreign dynasties including the Seljucian, Parthians, and Sassanians rule the country.
637 A.D.	The Arabs invade and assume control of Mesopotamia. The ancient city of Basra, located at the head of the Persian Gulf, is founded. Because of its strategic location, Basra becomes a cultural center of literature and religion. The majority of the population convert to Islam.
750 A.D.	Arab-Islamic civilization passes from the Syrian Omayyad's to the Abbasid who took over the Caliphates.
766 A. D.	Baghdad is founded by the second Caliph Abu Jafer Al-Mansour and becomes the capital. It is called the City of Peace (Dar Al-Salam).
1258 A.D.	The Mongols invade and destroy Baghdad and its civilization. Mesopotamia plunges into dark ages.
1532 A.D.	The Ottoman Empire takes control of Mesopotamia. It will rule for almost 400 years, until the end of the First World War.
1845–1851	Sir Austen Henry Layard excavates Nimrud and unearths the winged lions and the remains of Assyrian palaces. In 1849 he finds the ancient city of Nineveh, the palace of Senharib, and thousands of cuneiform tablets. Hermoz Rassam, an Iraqi from the city of Mosul who assisted Sir Layard, is appointed by the British Museum to continue excavation on its behalf. He discovers the Lion-Hunt relief of Ashur Banipal, and the remainder of the clay tablets library including the Epic of Gilgamesh.

1891	Basra becomes the principal port of Iraq and transshipment point for river traffic to Baghdad. The growth of Iraq's petroleum industry turns Basra into a major oil refining center.
1899–1913	German archaeologist Robert Koldewey works in Babylon and uncovers the foundation of the Babylonian God Mardukh's temple, a ziggurat and the fabled Hanging Gardens.
1914	At the outbreak of World War I, Great Britain occupies Basra, located at the head of the Persian Gulf to protect its oil interests. (Under the Ottomans, the Tigris and Euphrates valley was divided into three main provinces (*wilayat*): Mosul, Baghdad, and Basra.)
1917–1918	British Army defeats the Ottoman Empire and seizes Baghdad. Later the British move into Mosul and occupy the oil fields.
1920	Britain is given the mandate to create the state of Iraq with approval from the League of Nations. A new state with a modern government is established along with creation of the country and defined boundaries that stir problems with the Kurdish region and its neighbors. Great Iraqi rebellion against the British rule ensues.
1921	King Faisal I, the son of Hussein Bin Ali, the Sharif of Mecca, is crowned as Iraq's first king.
1925	The boundaries for the modern state of Iraq are established.
1932	Iraq becomes an independent state.
1939–1945	World War II is fought and Britain reoccupies Iraq.
1958	The Iraqi monarchy is overthrown in a military coup by Abdul Karim Qassim and Abdul Salam Muhammad Arif. Iraq is declared a republic.
1963	A coup is led by the Socialist Baathist party and Abdul Salam Muhammad Arif becomes president.
1968	A Baathist coup ousts Arif and the Revolutionary Command Council takes charge with Ahmad Hassan Al-Bakr at its head.
1970	Mulla Mustaf Al-Barazani, the leader of the Kurdish Democratic Party, signs a peace agreement with the central government.
1972	Iraq nationalizes the oil industry.
1974	The Iraqi government grants limited autonomy to Kurdistan.
1979	Saddam Hussein succeeds Al-Bakr as president.
1980	Iran-Iraq war begins.
1988	Saddam Hussein orders a chemical attack on the Kurds. The UN negotiates a cease-fire between Iraq and Iran and the war ends.
1990	Iraq invades Kuwait. The UN Security Council condemns the invasion and orders complete withdrawal. Saddam Hussein refuses; UN imposes international sanctions on Iraq.

1991	United States launches air attack on Iraq which starts war in the Persian Gulf.
1994	Iraqi National Assembly recognizes Kuwait's borders and its independence.
1996	Hussein accepts UN proposition called Oil for Food program; sanctions remain in place.
1998–2002	Iraq ends cooperation with Unscom, the agency in charge of overseeing the destruction of weapons of mass destruction (WMD). The U.S. launches Operation Desert Fox and targets air strikes to pressure Saddam Hussein to allow weapon inspectors into Iraq.
2003–2011	U.S.-led invasion topples Saddam Hussein and his government. UN security backs U.S.-led administration in Iraq and lifts economic sanctions. Insurgency, unrest, suicide bombing, and sectarian violence intensifies. U.S. hands sovereignty to interim Iraqi government headed by Prime Minster Iyad Allawi, followed by Nouri Al Maliki as vice-president, and Jalal Al-Talabani as the new president.

INTRODUCTION
IRAQI HISTORY & TRADITIONS

Lying between the Tigris and Euphrates, Iraq was referred to by the Greeks as "Mesopotamia" which means "the land between the two rivers." It is also called the "Cradle of Civilization" since it was where the Sumerian, Akkadian, Assyrian, and Babylonian civilizations thrived from 3100 B.C. to the fall of Babylon in 539 B.C.

In the early twentieth century, archeologists uncovered clay tablets and artifacts that show the influence of these civilizations on human development with writing systems, codes of law, the invention of the wheel and the plow, the use of herbs for medicinal purposes, and agriculture.

The Sumerians had elaborate canal and irrigation systems. They grew grains and grazed cattle and sheep. The marshes near the City of Ur (birthplace of Abraham) in the south were loaded with fish. They also provided reeds, grass, and mud to build homes. Sumer was the oldest city and dates back 6,000 years. The Sumerians traded their dates, grains, and textiles with the peoples in the area as far as Syria, Turkey, and India. They imported metals and stones for building materials. When the Sumerian civilization collapsed in 1700 B.C., King Hammurabi took over, renamed it Babylonia, and united the Assyrians and Babylonians into one nation.

In 612 B.C., the Chaldeans captured Nineveh, a city in the north that was the capital of the Assyrians. King Nabu-khodnassar ruled there for 40 years and restored the glory of Babylon. During that time he took over both Israel and Judah because the Jews were fighting on the side of the Assyrians. In 586 B.C., the Babylonians destroyed the First Temple, which had been built by Solomon, and took the rich and aristocratic Jews prisoner to Babylon. In 539 B.C., Babylon fell to King Darius of Persia. He gave the Jews permission to return to Judea and rebuild the temple, but most Jews chose to remain in Babylon. There were a series of foreign dynasties that ruled Mesopotamia including Alexander of Macedonia, Seljucians,

Parthians, and Sassanians, until the Arab Muslims invaded Mesopotamia in 637 A.D. At the time of the invasion, most of the population was Christian and they had to pay non-Muslim taxes to the invaders. Some of the Christians who were unable to pay these taxes eventually converted to Islam and intermarried with the Arabs. The Arab Islamic civilization flourished during the time of the Ummayad and the Abbasid rule (750–1258 A.D.). Many great cities were founded, including Kufa and Basra; Baghdad was the capital. During this era of the Abbasid caliphs rule in Baghdad, the culinary traditions of Persia influenced Iraqi and Arabian cuisines. Many of the meat and fruit stews and rice became permanent features in Arab cuisine. Seasonal vegetables and fruits were used in their cooking. They preserved grains and legumes by drying them. Meat was preserved in jars filled with lamb fat. Meats were dried, smoked, or salted for safekeeping, or they were cooked by roasting, boiling, or barbecuing.

In 1258, the Mongols, led by Genghis Khan, invaded the country and captured Baghdad. Mesopotamia plunged into the Dark Ages of ignorance and poverty until the 1400s. The Ottoman Turks took control in the sixteenth century, and their rule lasted until they were defeated in World War I. The League of Nations assigned Britain to define the territory of Iraq, and they paid little attention to natural boundaries and ethnic divisions. They set up a government and installed a monarchy that ruled until 1958, when it was overthrown and Iraq was declared a republic. The following years were plagued with political instabilities until 1968 when the Baath party came to power and ruled until 2003.

During Mesopotamian rule, farmers cultivated the land and planted wheat, millet, barley, lentils, beans, and sesame seeds. Wheat became a key food in Babylon. They made unleavened bread from it (*khubz*) which is still a staple in the Iraqi diet. Wheat also provided the material for brewing beer. Rice was first imported from Persia in the first millennium.

Onions, garlic, lettuce, leeks, and cucumbers are the vegetables most often mentioned in the ancient clay tablets. The food was seasoned with aromatic seeds such as cumin, coriander, mustard, and sesame seeds. Pistachios and almonds were cultivated in the foothills of the north. Olives were cultivated in Nineveh. The Assyrians in the north introduced the cotton "wool bearing tree."

Date palm trees were cultivated in lower Mesopotamia where the weather is warm. Dates were a source of sugar and nutrition that was easy to store and preserve. The date palm tree also provided wood and fiber for making ropes. The date palm tree is still the Iraqi national tree.

Fruits such as pomegranates, apples, figs, pears, apricots, and grapes were known to grow in Mesopotamia. Fermented beverages like beer and wine that were consumed during religious banquets were produced using wheat, dates, and grapes.

Animals provided meat, milk, and cheese. In ancient Mesopotamia, they used to inflate internal organs and sheep skin to use as storage sacks for food while traveling. When milk was stored in the sheep's stomach, it interacted with the rennet and created cheese by accident. Even in modern times, cheese, dates, and bread are staples of the daily diet of desert dwellers and villagers.

Religion and Demographics

Baghdad is the capital of Iraq, located in the central plains. The west of Iraq is a hot desert. The third biggest city is the port of Basra located in the south and bordered by Kuwait and Saudi Arabia. The climate has always influenced the lives and diets of the many ethnic groups throughout Iraq. Due to oil production and economic prosperity during the 1970s, a large number of the rural population migrated toward the urban centers for job opportunities. The government introduced a private property reform system that had a great impact on agriculture, since it used to be run on a feudal system controlled by sheikhs who provided spiritual, legal, and tribal leadership. The government set up land reform to bridge the gap between the rich and poor and formed the Agricultural Service Cooperative and provided loans and recourses to farmers for mechanization and poultry and dairy projects. These projects faced severe obstacles under Saddam Hussein's policies. Improvements and resources did not reach the farmers. In 1981, the government abolished the collective farming program and privatized the agricultural industry which resulted in the reduction of farm production due to poor maintenance, sanitation, and shortage of labor. Under the UN Oil for Food program, and during the economic sanctions against Iraq

The three Mesopotamian cuneiform tablets on display at Yale University contain recipes in Akkadian that comprise the first cookbook and the first written recipes. Probably originating from southern Mesopotamia in the seventeenth century BC, these are the oldest known food recipes anywhere in the world. (Courtesy of Yale University Library, Babylonian Collection)

from 1997 to 2003, farm production reduced despite the abundance of water and land resources. Iraq imported large quantities of grains, fruit, meat, poultry, and dairy products from neighboring countries. Consumers began to hoard food and fill their freezers with imported beef and chicken to prepare for the food shortages in the market. Food and other imports were rationed. I remember standing in line to receive the weekly ration of two imported Bulgarian frozen chickens and a carton of eggs during the 1970s and 1980s. People with political influences were able to receive boxes of frozen chicken and meat. It became our pre-occupation to drive through the neighborhoods to check for the availability of food items to purchase. These were hard years that I remember living in Iraq. Rebuilding Iraq's agriculture now is a major priority. Investment and technical resources are planned to revitalize agriculture and food production to maintain Iraq's agricultural heritage.

Crude oil, refineries, petroleum products, and natural gas are the most important industries in Iraq. Other small manufacturing, food processing, textiles, and mining are flourishing too. Iraq exports dates, petroleum, and natural gas to neighboring countries and other major trade partners such as Russia, France, Brazil, and Japan.

Modern Iraq is a land of many religions and minority groups that coexist as an integral part of the Iraqi nation. The northern part of Iraq is the land of the Kurds, a main ethnic minority group living in Iraq, Syria, Turkey, and Iran. They are the second largest ethnic group living in the mountains and valleys of the north where they experience very harsh winters. They occupy Sulymaniya, Arbil, and Duhok provinces in an area referred to as Kurdistan. The Kurds have their own language, culture, and self government. The majority of ethnic minorities, such as the Turkomans, Assyrians, Chaldeans, and Syrians, live in the northern Kurdish villages, Mosul, and Baghdad. They are affiliated with the Syrian Orthodox and Syrian Catholic churches. A small Mandean minority live in the southern cities of Iraq and in Baghdad. They speak Mandaic which is related to Aramaic.

The majority of the population (about 90 percent) are Muslims who identify with the Arab culture. Islam is the official religion of Iraq. There are five pillars of Islam: Profession of faith, praying five times per day, alms-giving, fasting, and pilgrimage to Mecca. Muslims are called to prayers by the *Muathin*, or attend the prayers led by the Imams at the mosques. Muslims gather at mosques every Friday for afternoon prayers led by the *Mulla* or *Imam*. Iraqi Muslims are split into two groups, the Sunnis who are the minority in Iraq, and the Shias who are the majority. The main difference between these sects is the conflict regarding the rightful heir to the Muslim authority after the death of Prophet Mohammed in the year 623. The Sunnis believe that Imam Abu Bakr was Mohammed's rightful successor while the Shias believe that Imam Ali, the cousin and son-in-law of the prophet, was the rightful successor.

During the holy month of Ramadan, all Muslims gather in homes to participate in reading the Quran. They abstain from food, drink, and pleasurable activities during daylight hours. At night they break the fast with dates, followed by a soup called *tashreeb* or *thireed*, which is dry slices of bread soaked in meat and vegetable stock. The choice of meat is chicken, lamb, and beef. Consumption of pork is forbidden due to religious reasons. Women spend hours in the kitchen preparing festive meals every night and invite relatives and neighbors to share those meals. After a month of fasting, they celebrate *Id Al Fitr*. They also celebrate *Id Al Adha*, honoring the return of the pilgrims from Al-Haj to Mecca, and they sacrifice a lamb for the occasion. The celebration lasts for three days. People visit their neighbors and relatives to wish them a happy feast. They dress up and take children to the amusement parks. They cook the whole lamb and serve it on a bed of rice. Grains, vegetable stews, and fruits are served. They invite neighbors to their home or send a plate of food or *klecha* cookies to their neighbors. This has also become an occasion to exchange gifts and visit cemeteries to pay respects to departed relatives.

Iraqi Christians gather for Mass on Saturday evening or Sunday morning. They are organized under a bishop who lives in Mosul or Baghdad. Christians typically fast forty days for Lent and prepare vegetarian meals based on grains and seasonal vegetables. Meat and dairy products are not on the menu. During Easter, they prepare lamb and *kubba* dishes. They bake *klecha* and other desserts to share with relatives and visitors. Christmas and New Year's Day are celebrated too by going to church for the services and then returning home for a festive meal with relatives and friends.

In 1917 over 80,000 Jews lived in Baghdad, but currently only a handful of Jewish minorities still live in Iraq. In the early 20th century, Jews lived and worked with Muslims and formed a prosperous class of businessmen and scholars. They emigrated to Israel and other parts of the world after World War II because of the persecution they suffered in Iraq and political uprisings that were a result of the intensifying Zionist movement. The small minority of Jews that remains in Iraq practices Judaism and have their own language and dialect. They celebrate the traditional Jewish holy days of Rosh-Hashanah (the Jewish New Year), Yom Kippur, Hanukkah, and Passover with traditional foods and meals.

Most of the Kurdish people in Iraq are Muslims and a small minority of them are Christians. Regardless of religion, Kurds celebrate the Nawroz (New Day) holiday on March 21st to welcome the Spring Equinox New Year and the beginning of spring. On this day about 2,500 years ago, a Kurdish blacksmith named Kawa, who lost his son as a sacrifice to Zahhak's serpent, liberated his people from the tyrant oppressor called Zahhak. Therefore Nawroz is considered the most important feast for Kurds around the world. Other nations such as Iran, Afghanistan, and Kazakhstan celebrate

Picnic in Kurdistan, North Iraq

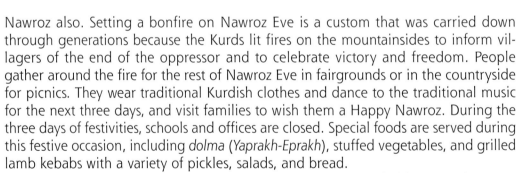

Nawroz also. Setting a bonfire on Nawroz Eve is a custom that was carried down through generations because the Kurds lit fires on the mountainsides to inform villagers of the end of the oppressor and to celebrate victory and freedom. People gather around the fire for the rest of Nawroz Eve in fairgrounds or in the countryside for picnics. They wear traditional Kurdish clothes and dance to the traditional music for the next three days, and visit families to wish them a Happy Nawroz. During the three days of festivities, schools and offices are closed. Special foods are served during this festive occasion, including *dolma* (*Yaprakh-Eprakh*), stuffed vegetables, and grilled lamb kebabs with a variety of pickles, salads, and bread.

The remaining ethnic groups include Assyrians, Armenians, Chaldeans, and Syrians, who are mainly Christians. There are five Christian churches: Chaldean, Nestorian, Jacobites (Syrian Orthodox), Syrian Catholic, and new Evangelical. Yazidis, who are a small minority in the north, are of Kurdish descent and practice their unique religion that combines paganism, Zoroastrianism, Christianity, and Islam. A small minority of Mandean or Sabaean, who are the followers of John the Baptist, live in southern Iraq and in Baghdad. They pray three times a day in Aramaic, a language close to the one spoken by Jesus Christ. Mandean leaders estimate that there are as few as 10,000 of their followers remaining in Iraq, with small groups in other countries around the world.

All Iraqis speak and understand Arabic, the official language of Iraq, which is of Semitic origin. The Kurdish language is of Indo-European origin. The other minority languages are Aramaic, Turkic, Armenian, Hebrew, and Persian.

Family Life

In Iraq arranged marriages are very common, although in urban settings women and men have more options in choosing their spouses with their parents' approval. In the Muslim tradition, marriage to a cousin is preferred, and marriage to the first cousin is supposed to be the perfect match. Marriage outside the family is a last resort. A young person who marries without the parents' consent is expelled from the family and the clan. When a match is approved outside the family, parents on both sides do detective work on the respective spouse and their family. Whether the family is a good match financially and socially, and whether the gentleman and the young lady have good reputations and a good job are taken into consideration. The groom and his parents ask for the girl's hand in marriage, and when the young lady says yes, they begin to plan for the engagement (*al Khitooba* or *Nishan*) ceremony. Gold is important, and the quantity of gold presented to the bride shows the groom's appreciation and family wealth. The bride and the groom begin planning and shopping for their wedding day. The parents on both sides share the expenses of the wedding. The groom's family provides an

My parents, aunts, brother, and sisters in the garden, 1960

engagement ring for both the bride and groom, and the party is held by the young lady's family in their home or in a night club, inviting their relatives and friends. A long period of socializing follows, and getting to know each other chaperoned by an immediate family member.

On her wedding day, the bride is dressed in a western-style wedding dress and wears the gold jewelry given to her by the groom. According to the Muslim tradition, the bride as well as female members of the immediate family have their hands and feet decorated with henna on the day before the wedding (called *Laylat il Henna*, the Night of Henna). On the wedding day, the groom arrives at the bride's home with a religious leader to sign the contract while the immediate family and friends are present. The bride and groom and their noisy, horn-blowing families and friends take a convoy of buses and cars (*zaffa*) through the streets to the groom's house or to a dance hall or hotel ballroom for the reception. Men and women are segregated during the celebrations, especially in the countryside where they would have separate tents, food, and entertainment.

For Christians in Iraq, the wedding ceremony is very close to western wedding ceremonies, and is held in a church. After church, everybody is invited to a reception in the church hall, a club, or a hotel ballroom. All food is catered and a DJ with music is provided, and men and women participate together in dancing all night. Although some Christian marriages are arranged through friends and relatives, the females are never forced into a marriage or into marrying a cousin, which is forbidden by the church. If some Christian families arrange for cousins to marry each other to keep the wealth in the family, they would typically have to go outside their church to get married. Divorces are discouraged by the church, and remarrying is frowned upon. A Christian divorced woman would not be able to get remarried, while in the Muslim communities, it is much easier for divorced women to remarry, most likely to a cousin.

Marriages between the different ethnic groups are accepted, but not very common. The couple can live with the husband's family if they experience economic hardships. Sometimes, the family builds an apartment attached to their home for the bride and groom to occupy and take care of the seniors in the family.

A few weeks after a baby is born, Christians take the child to church to get baptized to admit him or her to the Christian faith. Family and friends are invited to pay their respects with gifts and money, and a table of sweets is set for the

My nephew's wedding in a church in Baghdad

My nephew's son's baptism in Baghdad

visitors. Small wrapped candy treats are given out at the baptism. After the ceremony, the guests attend a reception in the church hall or at home. They all gather to celebrate the christening feast with food and drinks, singing and dancing while the infant is put to bed.

Circumcision for Muslim boys is an important event. Some are circumcised in the hospital after they are born. When the mother returns home with the baby, a small family dinner celebrates the event. In the countryside they circumcise children when they reach the age of seven and then there is a parade through the village with music and dance, and everybody is invited for a feast which is traditionally roasted lamb over a big tray of rice and a stew on the side. Big trays of baklava and sweets are served too.

Grandparents and aunts live with the older son and his family. The older son usually makes the final decisions regarding the children's education, their spouses, and finances. Many couples prefer to live in their own households if they can afford it. The family holds an important role in teaching values, duty, and responsibility. Obedience and loyalty to elders are very important. Unfortunately, there is rejoicing over the birth of a boy but not over the birth of a girl. Boys have more freedom and authority while girls have to submit to too many restrictions and customs. Men inherit twice as much as women since the man is the main provider for the family. Women do not enjoy the same social rights and privileges as men, and any reform has to follow the Islamic Law.

Meals served at weddings, celebrations, and funerals are very important. These meals are served in big halls or in gardens, sometimes under big tents. Guests have the choice of sitting at a table and eating with a fork and a spoon or squatting on the

Feast at church hall following baptism

floor and eating with the fingers of their right hands. These meals are elaborate and indicate the economic status of the host. Traditional dishes are grilled lamb and chicken served over a big bed of rice, trays of grilled fish, vegetable stews, and trays of fruits and sweets. Rice dishes are served from a big tray, but stews are served in individual bowls. Each guest eats from the part of the tray nearest to him or her. They use three fingers of their right hands instead of a spoon, but many guests do prefer to use spoons instead. Feasts are also prepared during Eid Al-Adha and Ramadan for the family and visiting friends and relatives. During the holiday celebrations, it is traditional to sacrifice a lamb and distribute the meat to the neighbors or to the poor in the mosque.

Another occasion for preparing and distributing food is the funeral ceremony. Upon a death, relatives and neighbors prepare food at the home of the deceased or bring it to the home for three days following the burial ceremony to serve the guests making condolence visits. Guests are also served bitter coffee and tea. Those visiting in the afternoon are served a big meal. Men and women receive their guests in separate rooms. Visitors bring sacks of rice, tea, sugar, and other gifts as a gesture of support for the family.

Influences on the Iraqi Cuisine

The recipes in this book reflect the cuisine with which I grew up and come from all parts of Iraq. The northern region of Iraq was influenced by Turkish cuisine. The recipes from the middle and southern regions of the country were influenced by the Persians, who made their pilgrimage to Karbala from Iran, and the Indian spice route that came through the port city of Basra in the south.

In the early 1970s, many Lebanese families settled in Iraq to escape the civil war in Lebanon. These families brought their cuisine with them and introduced the tabouli salad, *hummus bithini*, pita bread, and *laham ajeen*, similar to a meat pizza, and a thyme bread called *manaqeesh* or *zaatar* bread. During the 1980s, three million Egyptians came to Iraq to fill the positions of the Iraqi men fighting the war with Iran. They brought falafel, *foul mudamas* (boiled fava beans), and *milukhiya* soup. There is a large population of Palestinians who settled in Baghdad. Their cuisine is very similar to the Lebanese and they influenced the Iraqi cuisine with their special desserts and pastries filled with spinach, cheese, and meat.

These are just a few examples of dishes and delicacies that were introduced to the Iraqi menu in restaurants, served on the street food carts, and enjoyed during celebrations.

STREET FOOD

Street food in Iraq is a quick meal or snack sold by sidewalk vendors from push-carts, baskets carried on their heads, or stalls by store fronts. I always remember the sesame bagel (*simeet*) vendor, and the roasted peanuts vendor by the university entrance. Some vendors sell hot snacks such as fava bean stew (*bajilla*), chickpea stew (*lablabi*), boiled turnips (*shalgham*), *kubba*, eggs, tomato and pickled mango sandwiches, and lamb kabab (*tikka*) sandwiches. You can find these street carts everywhere, and their success depends on location and word of mouth.

Some permanent stalls sell yogurt drinks (*shinina*) and fruit juices such as pomegranate juice (*sharab rumman*) and raisin drinks (*sharbat zibib*) during the summer. Tea and coffee stalls are very popular for every season.

Most vendors are people who lack the education necessary to hold an office job, or who operate a cart as a second job due to economic hardship. Many of them are young men, women, and children who sell food on the streets to support their families. This is a vital part of the economy, and selling the food they grow or make is an important way to earn income. Although there are concerns for cleanliness, hygiene, and freshness, these vendors provide cheap meals to thousands of people who otherwise would not be able to afford a better meal or snack.

Left page, current photos of Baghdad street vendors—*top left*: boiled chickpeas cart; *top right*: fruit shop; *bottom left*: lettuce and vegetables shop; *bottom right*: watermelon vendor under tent; *center*: Simeet vendor carrying a tray of *simeet* on his head.

SPICES & HERBS

Spices and flavorings are at the heart of the Iraqi cuisine. The art of using spices to flavor the meal or using spices for medicinal purposes is passed down from grandmothers and mothers. Sometimes the terms for herbs and spices are used interchangeably, but it is important that we clarify these definitions. Spices are parts (dried seeds, buds, stems, fruit, bark, flower, root) of tropical aromatic plants, such as cloves, cinnamon, cardamom, ginger, and allspice; while herbs are the leafy parts of a plant, such as parsley, mint, thyme, sage, rosemary, and dill.

It is important to learn how to buy, store, and use these herbs and spices. Using fresh herbs is best when possible, but I use dry mint, parsley, and dill in my recipes during winter. Rinse the fresh herbs in several changes of water, especially if you find particles of sand in the water, and drain them in a colander. Pat them dry with paper towel and then wrap them in a paper towel and store in a Ziploc bag in the refrigerator for up to four days. To dry the herbs, you can spread them on a tray and keep them on the kitchen counter or in an airy room for a few days. You could also put the tray outdoors to dry out of direct sunlight for a day or two. When the colors fade a little and the herbs become brittle, then you know they are dry. Put them in a jar or a plastic bag with a date, and label and store in your cupboard. When fresh herbs are not available, substitute one part dried for three parts fresh. The dried herbs have more potent flavor than the fresh because the water has been removed. Crush the dried herbs in the palm of your hands to release the flavor and add them to the soups towards the end of cooking, to the rice while boiling, and to salads. Dried herbs will last 6 months to a year when stored in a cool and dark area of the kitchen.

Spices are best when freshly ground. Use a peppermill or a coffee grinder for this purpose. We usually use the mortar and pestle to crush the whole spices and then put them in a coffee grinder. Grind a small quantity at a time and store in small jars. When spices get old, they lose their potency. You can sniff them or taste a pinch to check the flavor and aroma. If they have lost their potency, you can either double the amount you use for the recipe, or discard and grind a new batch. Store them in a clean container in a dark, cool area of your kitchen and they will last for a year. Whole spices can last a few years.

ARABIAN SPICE   BAHAR

This is a special family spice blend recipe used in many of the recipes in this book. We used to go to a special bazaar, Shourja Market, in Baghdad where many vendors sell spices. We would ask the shop owner to measure these spices and grind them for us. Spice shops do have the Arabian Spice already ground, but Mother preferred to have her spices freshly ground. She kept the ground spice blend in a tightly closed jar.

½ cup whole black peppercorns

1 cup whole cinnamon sticks

1 cup whole allspice

10 cardamom pods

10 cloves

3 pieces (1-inch each) dry ginger root

½ cup dried rose petals (optional)

1 whole nutmeg

Crush these spices with mortar and pestle before grinding them in a coffee grinder. Store in an airtight container.

Use the following recipe if you just need a small amount of Arabian Spice. It uses already ground spices so is quicker to assemble.

1 tablespoon ground black pepper

2 tablespoons ground allspice

2 tablespoons ground cinnamon

1 teaspoon ground cloves

1 teaspoon ground cardamom

½ teaspoon ground nutmeg

½ teaspoon ground ginger

A version of this spice blend, also called Syrian Spice or Seven Spices, can be purchased ready-mixed at Middle Eastern grocery stores (though it won't be our special family blend).

Mix all the above spices and store them in a tightly closed jar.

Below I have listed some of the herbs and spices commonly used in Iraqi recipes, and would recommend reading this list before you start using the recipes in this book.

Anise seeds – *Yansoon*
Use ground anise to flavor cookies and breads. We also use anise seeds for making tea. Bring 2 cups of water to a boil and add 2 tablespoons of anise seeds. Cover and steep for ten minutes. Strain and add sugar if you like. We prepare this tea for babies with colic.

Arabian Spice – *Bahar*
This is a spice blend used frequently in Iraq and in most of the savory recipes in this book. It is available pre-mixed in spice markets in Iraq but many cooks, including my mother, have their own version of it that they mix themselves. A recipe for it is given on the opposite page. I would recommend that you make up this spice blend ahead of time and keep some ready in your spice cupboard.

Arak – *Araq*
This is a very strong, dry, alcoholic drink distilled from grapes and flavored with anise seed. It has the pleasing flavor of licorice. Adults drink it straight or diluted with water and ice, which makes it become cloudy white. It is used to relieve an upset stomach.

Chamomile – *Bayboun*
We use the chamomile flower to make tea to treat cold symptoms: Bring 3 cups of water to a boil and add ½ cup of chamomile flowers. Bring to a boil again and remove from heat. Leave the teapot covered for ten minutes to steep. Strain into a cup and add honey.

Cardamom – *Hail*
Cardamoms are small green pods that contain tiny brown seeds. It is sold as pods, seeds, and powder. Grind whole cardamom pods and seeds together as needed and keep in a jar. I use whole cardamom pods to flavor chicken and beef stews, and the ground cardamom to flavor Arabic coffee and tea. I add ground cardamom to cookies and cakes for flavoring.

Cumin – *Kammun*
Ground cumin is one of the ingredients used in lentil soup and for making *basturma*, a breakfast sausage.

Dried Lime – *Noomi Basra*
Dried limes give a tart flavor to stews. You can also buy them ground and add 1 tablespoon to chicken or beef stew. We use the whole dried lime to make tea (*Chai Hamuth*): Crush the whole lime and remove the seeds. Add to a pot of boiling water; boil for ten minutes and then steep for ten more minutes. Pour into a cup using a strainer and add sugar. Serve this tea for upset stomachs.

Nigella seeds (Black seeds) – *Habbat Soda*
These black seeds have a peppery flavor and are very popular ingredients in breads and *klecha* cookies.

Rose Petals – *Jinbud, Warid*

We harvest rose petals during the summer to make jam. Make sure they are organic and not treated with pesticides. Dried rose petals are ground and added to the pepper blend Arabian Spice. We also boil them to make tasty and aromatic tea.

Rose Water – *Mai Warid*

Rose water is distilled and sold in bottles in Middle Eastern markets. Add it to flavor custards, rice pudding, syrups, and cookies.

Saffron – *Zaafaran*

Saffron is the stigma of the crocus flower. There are different varieties of saffron and variance in prices too. It gives a unique flavor and yellow color to rice dishes. Put ¼ teaspoon of saffron in a cup of boiling water. Cover to steep and add it to rice while cooking or to chicken stew.

Summac – *Summaq*

This spice gives a sour and lemony flavor and is used as a condiment. Ground summac has a reddish color and is sprinkled over kabab or rice. Whole dried summac berries are rarely found in grocery stores outside the Middle East. We soak these berries in hot water, strain them, and use the liquid to flavor okra, *dolma*, and stuffed grape leaves.

Tamarind – *Tamir Hind*

Tamarind is used to flavor soups and stews. It is tart and has a sweet and sour flavor. You can purchase ready-to-use tamarind paste in a jar. I prefer to use the dried bean pods. Peel the pods and soak the pulp in hot water. Stir and discard the seeds. Strain and freeze the juice in small containers. When ready to use, add to rice *kibbi* soup, okra stew, and *dolma*. In the summer, we mix the pulp with sugar, add ice, and drink it as *Sharbat Tamir Hind*— very refreshing.

Turmeric – *Curcum*

This ground spice is used to add a bright yellow color to rice, and sometimes we add it to bread dough.

Water Mint – *Butnij*

Water mint is crossed with spearmint to create a new peppermint plant. It grows in shallow areas of water. Unlike mint, this plant is pollinated by insects. Dried *butnij* is sprinkled over fava beans and salads.

> **Spices commonly used for baking in Iraq are ground cardamom, ground fennel, ground cinnamon, ground anise seeds, and whole nigella seeds. These spices are not blended together but used as indicated in the recipe.**
>
> **Spices used for pickling in Iraq are a combination of whole coriander, turmeric, curry powder, chili peppers, and bay leaf.**

IRAQI KITCHEN TOOLS

In the past, Iraqis used pottery urns and pots to cook over fire. Later, they used copper pots and pans and had an artisan come to the house to treat and cover the surface of the pots. For baking bread, they used a *tannour*, a wood-burning pottery oven with the shape of a huge urn that was 4 feet high with a 20-inch circular opening on top.

For heating, Iraqis used a *manqal*, a flat aluminum tray supported by four legs. They put hot coals on top to heat the space. Usually they had a kettle on top of the fire and a teapot sitting on top of the kettle. *Manqals* are still used to grill kababs outdoors. A *primus*, a single kerosene pressure stove, is a very popular and mobile unit used for cooking and boiling water for washing and bathing. With a gas tank and burner attached it became more popular to use for picnics and cooking indoors and outdoors.

Iraqis use a brass mortar and pestle (*hawan*) to crush spices and grains. They also have used it to pound meat with bulgur to make *kibbi*. A manual meat grinder is used for this purpose also but nowadays we often use food processors. At the present time, the Iraqi home and kitchen is equipped with modern cooking tools and appliances imported from all over the world. The Iraqi manufacturing industry produces gas stoves, refrigerators, air conditioners, and other small appliances, but they cannot keep up with the demands of the consumers.

Tannour bread bakery

APPETIZERS
&
PICKLES

Appetizers

When I was growing up and we had guests invited to dinner, everyone went to the table when an announcement was made that the dinner was ready. Dinner was served with breads, salads, pickles, heavy appetizers such as *potato chap* and *kibbat halab*, and soups. This wide range of foods, including appetizers and main dishes both hot and cold, appeared on the table at the same time. At the end of the meal, fruit and puddings were served, followed by tea (*chai*) and desserts.

Serving appetizers before the meal became popular with the boom of the restaurant and club industry in the late 1960s. We adopted the tradition at home, serving appetizers with beer and *arak* before the main meal. In the homes where alcoholic drinks are not served, they serve tea or *sharbat* juice drinks before serving the meal.

An appetizer menu typically includes: boiled chickpeas, boiled fava beans, Arabic salad or sliced tomatoes and cucumbers, pickles and olives, boiled eggs, *basturma* sausage, *tikka* lamb kabab chunks on skewers, *kufta* kabab, pistachios and mixed nuts. Some heavy appetizers are also served, such as the potato *chap* and *kibbat halab*, and grilled lamb liver and kidneys served with *tannour* bread.

Pickles (Turshi)

Pickles are a very important part of an Iraqi meal. During the summer, we pickle cucumbers, green peppers, eggplants, and green beans. During winter, we pickle cabbage, cauliflower, carrots, turnips, and beets. Sometimes we add slices of apples or pears to the mixture. There are basically two methods for pickling: salt brine or vinegar mixture. We always made our natural vinegars from dates or grapes, but commercially prepared apple cider vinegar or wine vinegars work well, too.

PICKLED CUCUMBERS

TURSHI KHIAR

VINEGAR METHOD

Ingredients

4 cups apple cider vinegar

2 teaspoons ground coriander

1 teaspoon curry powder

4 cloves garlic, sliced

⅓ cup kosher salt

5 pounds small cucumbers

Preparation

Place vinegar, spices, garlic, and salt in a pot and bring to a boil. Remove from heat and drop the cucumbers in the hot vinegar and allow to sit for 5 minutes to blanch.

Remove cucumbers from vinegar and stack in a big sterilized jar. When vinegar cools, pour over the cucumbers and close the jar. The pickles should be ready to eat within 3 days.

Store jars in the refrigerator after opening.

SALT BRINE METHOD

Ingredients

5 pounds small cucumbers

1 cup kosher salt, divided

5 cloves garlic, sliced

1 tablespoon sugar

Note: With salt brine, you will notice white scum develops on the surface of the brine due to fermentation. Skim the scum regularly and make sure the vegetables are well covered by the brine.

Preparation

Wash cucumbers and poke holes in them with a knife. Sprinkle ⅓ cup of salt over them and leave for a few hours in a colander to wilt.

Place the cucumbers and garlic in a few sterilized jars. Add sugar and the remaining salt. Pour in enough filtered water to come to the top of jars. Cover jars and leave for 10 days, until the cucumbers change color.

Store jars in the refrigerator after opening.

PICKLED STUFFED EGGPLANTS

TURSHI BADINJAN

You can purchase baby eggplants from Asian and Middle Eastern grocery stores. Make sure the stems are green and the skin is glossy.

Ingredients

10 baby eggplants

4 to 5 cups apple cider vinegar

½ cup salt

1 tablespoon curry powder

1 head garlic, chopped

1 cup chopped fresh Italian parsley

1 tablespoon ground coriander

Note: You can use this same recipe for stuffed green peppers.

Preparation

Wash eggplants and split in half lengthwise up to but not including the stem. Make sure to keep the eggplants attached to the stem.

In a large pot, bring the vinegar to a boil with salt and curry powder and then remove from heat. Drop the eggplants in the hot vinegar mixture and allow to sit for 30 minutes to wilt. Remove the eggplants from the vinegar and place in a colander to drain. Reserve vinegar mixture.

In a small bowl, combine garlic, parsley, and coriander. Stuff the insides of the eggplants with this mixture. Tie each whole eggplant with a cord or with one long Italian parsley sprig with a long stem so the two halves stay together.

Arrange the eggplants in a sterilized jar and pour the vinegar and salt mixture over them. Make sure they are completely covered by the vinegar.

Seal the jar tightly and leave for 14 days. Refrigerate after opening.

CAULIFLOWER PICKLES
TURSHI QARNABEET

Ingredients

1 head (2 pounds) cauliflower
5 cloves garlic
⅓ cup kosher salt
1 tablespoon curry powder (optional)
3 cups apple cider vinegar

Preparation

Wash cauliflower and cut into small florets. Place in a pot of boiling water and cook for 15 minutes. Remove from the pot and place in a colander to drain.

Arrange the cauliflower in a sterilized jar along with the garlic, salt, and curry powder.

Pour the vinegar to the top of the jar. Cover the jar and leave for 4 days before serving.

Store in the refrigerator after opening.

PICKLED TURNIPS
MUKHALALA

Ingredients

5 pounds turnips
1 pound fresh beets, sliced
¾ cup kosher salt
About 12 cups water or apple cider vinegar
Chopped fresh parsley for decoration

Preparation

Wash the turnips, cut off the ends, and make a deep slit in the center of each turnip while keeping the two halves attached, or you could slice the turnips in ½-inch slices. Slice the beets and layer the beets and turnips in a big sterilized jar or a big pottery urn, adding salt to each layer.

Pour in enough water or apple cider vinegar to cover the turnips. Seal the jar and leave for 10 days. Top with chopped parsley when serving.

FRIED RICE KIBBI

KIBBAT HALAB

This is a torpedo-shaped rice kibbi *filled with a meat and onion mixture (qeema). We take it to picnics or serve it as finger food or a light dinner with pickles.*

Ingredients

Dough:

3 cups cooked rice with saffron

3 small potatoes, boiled and peeled

½ teaspoons salt

Filling:

2 tablespoons vegetable oil, divided

1 pound ground chuck

1 medium onion, chopped

1 teaspoon salt

1 teaspoon Arabian Spice (page 22)

½ cup toasted almond slivers

½ cup raisins

½ cup chopped fresh Italian parsley

2 cups vegetable oil for frying

Preparation

Dough:
Put the cooked rice and potatoes in a food processor and add salt. Pulse a few times until it makes a soft ball.

Qeema Filling:
Heat 1 tablespoon of oil in a pan. Sauté the meat and onions. Add salt and spice blend and keep stirring until browned. Set aside. Sauté the almonds in remaining 1 tablespoon of oil until toasted. Add the raisins and stir for half a minute. Remove from heat and add to the meat mixture. Set aside to cool. When the filling is cool add the parsley and stir.

Assembly:
To form the *kibbi*, take a small piece of rice dough the size of an egg. Shape it into a cup and fill it with the meat mixture. Pinch the edges of the cup to enclose filling. Shape it like a large egg and place it on a tray. Repeat until all dough is used.
Heat the oil in a deep pan and deep fry the

kibbi for a few minutes until they are lightly browned. Drain on paper towels. When cool, freeze or refrigerate them. They can also be frozen before frying.

Serve the fried *kibbi* warm or at room temperature. To reheat them, place them on a baking pan and bake at 350 degrees F for 10 minutes. This will ensure a crunchy texture.

POTATO KIBBI

POTATO CHAP

This appetizer is potato patties stuffed with a meat or vegetarian filling and usually deep fried. You need to prepare the filling in advance and make sure it is cool before stuffing the potato dough.

Ingredients

Meat Filling:

2 teaspoons vegetable oil

1 pound ground chuck

1 medium onion, chopped

1 teaspoon Arabian Spice (page 22)

1 teaspoon salt

½ cup chopped parsley

Vegetarian Filling:

3 tablespoons olive oil

1 medium onion, chopped

½ pound sliced mushrooms

1 teaspoon salt

1 teaspoon Arabian Spice (page 22)

½ cup frozen peas

Potato Dough:

2 pounds potatoes, boiled and peeled

2 tablespoons cornstarch

1 egg

½ teaspoon salt

½ cup dry breadcrumbs, if needed

Preparation

Meat Filling:

Heat oil in a skillet and sauté ground chuck and onions. Add spice blend and salt. When cooked, add parsley. Set aside to cool. The filling must be cool before filling the potato dough.

Vegetarian Filling:

Heat oil in a skillet and sauté the onions. Add the mushrooms and season with salt and spice blend. Cook for 10 minutes until mushrooms are soft. Add the frozen peas and stir. Remove from heat and set aside to cool before stuffing the potato dough.

Potato Dough:

Put potatoes, cornstarch, egg, and salt in the food processor and pulse until well mixed. You can add breadcrumbs if the mixture is too moist.

Assembly:

To assemble, form the potato mixture into balls the size of an egg. Shape each ball into a cup and fill with meat or vegetarian mixture. Pinch the edges of the cup to enclose the filling and shape them into patties.

2 cups vegetable oil for frying

Heat oil to 300 degrees F. Drop in a few *kibbi*. Cook on both sides until golden brown. Remove and place on paper towels to drain. Cook remaining *kibbi* in the same manner. Serve warm or hot with pickles as an appetizer.

MEAT TURNOVERS
BOUREK / SANBOUSAK

10 servings

Traditionally we make bread dough and fill it with the meat mixture, and then fry the turnovers in oil. But you could use frozen bread dough for rolls (found in most freezer sections in grocery stores) for these turnovers. Defrost the rolls overnight in the refrigerator before you use them. I use phyllo dough for a lighter and easier version, and bake them in the oven.

Ingredients

Meat Filling:

2 teaspoons vegetable oil

1 pound ground chuck

1 medium onion, chopped

½ teaspoon Arabian Spice (page 22)

½ teaspoon salt

½ cup raisins

½ cup toasted almond slivers

1 package phyllo dough, thawed

1 cup melted butter

1 cup vegetable oil for frying (if you are not baking in the oven)

Variation: You can also make Cheese Turnovers (*Sanbousak bil Jibin*) using the same method. To make the filling, mix together 2 pounds crumbled Arabic or feta cheese, 2 eggs, 1 tablespoon dried mint, and ½ cup chopped parsley.

Preparation

Meat Filling:
Heat oil in a skillet and sauté meat. Add onions, spice blend, and salt. When browned, add raisins and almonds. Set aside to cool. The filling must be cool before using.

Assembly:
Preheat oven to 350 degrees F. Place the phyllo dough on a cutting board and cover with a kitchen towel to prevent drying. Place 1 sheet of phyllo on another cutting board and fold in half. Brush phyllo with melted butter. Place 2 tablespoons of the filling in the middle of the sheet at one short end. Fold end of phyllo over the filling. Turn sides of phyllo in towards the center, and roll phyllo in shape of an eggroll. Repeat with remaining phyllo and filling.

Arrange *bourek* on a baking pan with the seam sides down. Brush with melted butter and bake for 20 minutes.

LAMB FRITTERS

SHIFTAYAT IROOK

These are very delicious pancakes that are served as a light dinner with pickles or prepared for picnics. They are crunchy when you remove them from the frying pan. When they cool off, they become soft. You can always reheat them in the oven for a crunchy bite.

Ingredients

1 pound chopped lamb

1 small onion, chopped

½ cup chopped fresh Italian parsley

½ cup chopped scallions

2 eggs

½ cup all-purpose flour

1 teaspoon salt

1 teaspoon Arabian Spice (page 22)

2 tablespoons water

½ teaspoon baking powder

1 cup vegetable oil for frying

Preparation

Place the meat in a large bowl and add all the ingredients except the oil. Stir mixture with a spoon to make a soft batter the consistency of porridge, adding more water if needed.

Heat the oil in a skillet. Drop 2 tablespoons of the batter in the pan for each fritter and press them with the back of the spoon to flatten. Fry for 3 minutes on each side until golden brown. Remove fritters with a fork and drain on a paper towel. Repeat with remaining meat mixture.

Eat while warm and crispy. Once they cool, put them in a plastic container and freeze. Serve for lunch or as an appetizer.

LAMB BRAINS

MUKH

Lamb brains are very delicate and take a short time to cook. They can be served in a sandwich or on a bed of lettuce as an appetizer.

Ingredients

1 pound lamb brains

1 teaspoon whole allspice

1 stick cinnamon

4 whole cloves

1 small onion, sliced

Juice of ½ lemon, or 1 tablespoon
    vinegar

1 teaspoon salt

Preparation

Wash the lamb brains in cold water. Place them in a pot with enough water to cover. Add allspice, cinnamon, cloves, onion slices, lemon juice or vinegar, and salt. Bring to a boil and cook for 15 minutes.

Remove the brains gently from the pot to cool. Gently remove the filament covering the brains, making sure not to tear the brain. Place in the refrigerator until chilled. Slice before serving and serve cold on a bed of lettuce with pickles.

LAMB TONGUE

LISAN

Ingredients

2 pounds lamb tongue

1 teaspoon salt

1 teaspoon Arabian Spice (page 22)

Preparation

Place lamb tongue in a pot with enough water to cover. Add salt and spice blend. Bring to a boil and then reduce heat to medium. Cook for 90 minutes until tender. Remove from heat and cool.

When cool, peel the tongue, and slice it. Arrange slices on a bed of lettuce and serve as an appetizer.

Some dishes have been given the name of a body part or something in nature they resemble. This recipe has the name of Lady's Arm. There is an okra stew and a dessert both called Lady's Fingers. Another dessert made of phyllo is called Bird's Nest.

LADY'S ARM
ZAND IL KHATOON

My mother used to make this appetizer for New Year's Eve. She would pound the meat and keep mixing it by hand until it became like a paste. Luckily, it has become much easier to make since I started using the food processor for this purpose. This appetizer is served cold and goes very well with arak, an alcoholic drink that has an anisette flavor.

Ingredients

Meat Mixture:

½ pound lean ground beef or lamb

1 medium onion, chopped

2 tablespoons dry breadcrumbs

1 egg

2 cloves garlic, chopped

1 teaspoon salt

½ teaspoon ground cumin

½ teaspoon Arabian Spice (page 22)

Assembly:

3 hard-boiled eggs

1 tablespoon vegetable oil

Tomatoes and herbs for decoration

Variation: My sister Samar rolls this meat in foil and places it in a pot of boiling water. She adds whole spices and salt to the water and boils it for 25 minutes.

Preparation

Put all the ingredients for the meat mixture in a food processor and pulse until it becomes a paste. Remove from the processor and place in a bowl. Cover the bowl with plastic wrap and place in the refrigerator for 1 hour. This will allow the spices to blend with the meat.

Preheat the oven to 375 degrees F. Place a sheet of plastic wrap on a cutting board. Brush the plastic wrap with water. Place the meat mixture on top of the plastic wrap and roll it out to make an 8-inch square.

Peel the hard-boiled eggs and line them up on the center of the meat. Lift the plastic wrap and roll the meat over the eggs until they are covered. Seal the meat on all sides. Discard the plastic wrap.

Place the roll on aluminum foil and drizzle with oil. Wrap with foil and bake for 30 minutes. Remove from the oven and leave to cool for 15 minutes on the cutting board. Open the foil and let the steam escape. Place the roll in the refrigerator for a few hours before slicing. Serve with sliced tomatoes and fresh herbs.

ZUCCHINI FRITTERS

IROOK IL SHIJAR

These are special vegetarian pancakes prepared during Lent. They are best crispy, so eat them as soon as you remove them from the frying pan as they become soft as they cool. But you can warm them in the oven for ten minutes to re-crisp them if needed.

Ingredients

1 cup peeled and shredded zucchini

1 medium onion

½ teaspoon salt

5 tablespoons all-purpose flour

½ teaspoon baking powder

½ cup fresh breadcrumbs

1 teaspoon Arabian Spice (page 22)

½ cup chopped fresh dill or parsley

1 cup vegetable oil for frying

Variation: You can use the same recipe to make Cauliflower Fritters.

Preparation

Place the shredded zucchini in a bowl. Put the onion in the food processor and pulse 3 to 4 times and add to the zucchini mixture. Season with salt. Place the mixture in a colander for 30 minutes to drain. Squeeze the remaining water out and place mixture in a bowl.

Add the flour, baking powder, and bread-crumbs to the zucchini mixture and combine well. Season with the spice blend, add the dill, and stir. Place the mixture in a bowl, cover and let rest for 30 minutes.

Heat the oil in a deep pan. Cooking in batches, drop a tablespoon of the fritter mixture into the oil for each fritter. Press them with the spoon to flatten. Fry for 3 minutes on one side and then turn and fry until the other side is lightly browned. Remove fritters from pan and drain on a paper towel. Repeat with remaining zucchini mixture. Serve hot with pickles.

CHICKPEA PATTIES

IROOK IL HUMMUS

6 servings

You can use any kind of canned beans for this recipe. We make it most often during Lent.

Ingredients

2 (13-ounce) cans chickpeas, rinsed
   and drained

3 cloves garlic, chopped

1 small onion, chopped

⅓ cup chopped fresh dill

1 egg (optional)

1 teaspoon ground cumin

½ teaspoon Arabian Spice (page 22)

1 teaspoon salt

⅓ cup all-purpose flour plus extra for
   coating

1 cup vegetable oil for frying

Preparation

Put all the ingredients (except the flour for coating and oil for frying) in a food processor and pulse. When the mixture is finely chopped, place in a bowl.

Take 1 tablespoon of the bean mixture and drop it in a bowl of flour. Roll in flour and shape it like a patty. Repeat with rest of bean mixture.

Heat the oil in a sauté pan over medium heat. Cooking in batches, drop the patties in oil and cook for 5 minutes on each side until golden brown. Remove from the pan and place on a tray lined with a paper towel to drain. Serve hot with pickles and salads.

GRILLED LIVER KABABS

KABAD MISHWI

For this recipe you can use either lamb or beef liver. My mother had a special way of grilling liver. She inserted lamb fat between the pieces of liver to prevent them from drying. She also rolled a piece of caul fat (fatty membrane surrounding the internal organs) over the liver pieces on a skewer before putting them on the grill. An Iraqi grill is called a manqal. It is a metal box supported by four legs. Charcoal is placed in the bottom of the box and is fanned by a hand or electric fan.

Ingredients

1 pound lamb or beef liver

1 small onion, chopped

1 teaspoon salt

1 teaspoon Arabian Spice (page 22)

Preparation

Cut liver into 1-inch cubes and wash. Pat the cubes dry with a paper towel.

Put liver in a bowl and toss with onion, salt, and spice blend and marinate for 30 minutes.

Put liver on skewers and grill on a charcoal grill for 5 minutes on each side. Serve as an appetizer or on bread as a sandwich.

Street vendors do a brisk business in freshly grilled kababs. They thread a variety of meats such as pieces of liver, heart, and lamb on very thin metal skewers, place them on the grill, and fan the burning coals. When cooked, they slide the meats onto a slice of warm bread, add parsley, basil, and onions and roll the sandwich. These are delicious for breakfast, lunch, or a late night snack. I have fond memories of the rising smell of this grilled meat while strolling along the Tigris River (Abu Nawas Street).

GRILLED LAMB KIDNEYS

KALAWI / CHALAWI

2 servings

We traditionally use lamb kidneys for grilling. They are tender and take a very short time to cook.

Ingredients

4 lamb kidneys

½ teaspoon salt

½ teaspoon Arabian Spice (page 22)

1 small onion, chopped

Preparation

Cut each kidney in half and wash. Remove the fat attached to them. Add salt, spice blend, and chopped onion, and marinate the kidneys for 30 minutes.

Thread the pieces of kidney on skewers and cook on a charcoal grill for 3 minutes on each side. You can also sauté in vegetable oil in a pan if you prefer. Serve as an appetizer.

BEVERAGES

Beverages

Iraqis drink tea all day and street vendors are on every corner selling it. Tea and coffee are mediums of hospitality offered while doing business. When you go shopping, the store owner orders tea and serves as host while you are trying to make a decision on the purchase. Iraqis use loose tea leaves imported from India, Ceylon (Sri Lanka), and China. They infuse tea with cardamom or cinnamon. Tea and milk (*chai halib*) is served for breakfast. But black tea (*chai sada*) is always served after lunch and dinner. Teas are also served in the afternoon with cake, pastries, and sweets.

Coffee originated in Ethiopia and was introduced to Yemen in the fifteenth century. It became one of the most important necessities of life in the Middle East. Strong Arabic coffee is served any time of the day with or without sugar, and is offered on social and business occasions. Milk is never added but we infuse coffee with ground cardamom for a pleasing flavor. The coffee beans are imported from Yemen, Ethiopia, India, Colombia, and Brazil, and are available in shops that specialize in grinding and selling coffee to order. Sometimes we ask the shop to grind cardamom seeds with the coffee to make the distinctive sweet Arabic coffee.

Shinina, a yogurt drink, is always served with lunch or dinner. It is a combination of yogurt, water, and ice cubes with a pinch of salt. It is a very refreshing drink during the summer, and sold by street vendors too.

Iraq also produces carbonated sodas, beer, and wine. Imported juices and drinks are available in the markets also.

ARABIC COFFEE
QAHWI / GAHWA

2 servings

This is a very strong and thick coffee. It is offered to guests with a piece of candy and a glass of water. Use Colombian coffee and have it ground in a very fine Turkish ground. Add ground cardamom for an aromatic flavor. For real authenticity, brew it in a special Arabic coffee pot called a dala.

Ingredients

1 cup water

1 teaspoon sugar

2 teaspoons ground coffee

When guests finish drinking coffee, they flip the cup upside down on the saucer and wait for 5 minutes for any leftover black coffee drops to run down the sides of the cup onto the saucer, making designs on the walls of the demitasse. Then guests wait for someone in the house to read their fortunes for entertainment.

Preparation

Combine, water, sugar, and ground coffee in a coffee pot or *dala*. Place the coffee pot on the burner on top of the stove and stir. When it starts to boil and the coffee reaches the rim of the pot remove from the stove to avoid overflowing.

Skim off the foam and spoon it into small demitasses or espresso cups. Return the coffee pot to the stove and allow coffee to boil to the rim twice more. Pour carefully into the small demitasses or espresso cups. Do not stir as that would break the foam that rises to the top.

TEAS
CHAI

BASIC TEA   CHAI

My mother used to mix three brands of loose tea to get the flavor she liked. She also added cardamom pods or ground cardamom for flavoring.

Put 3 teaspoons tea leaves in a medium teapot and fill it three-quarters full with 3 cups boiling water. Place teapot on top of the kettle to keep warm in the steam and steep for 5 to 10 minutes. Pour tea in a demitasse cup (*istikan*) and add sugar. If the black tea is very strong and you prefer light tea, pour tea to half of *istikan* and add more boiling water.

TEA WITH MILK   CHAI HALIB

When I was growing up, a nearby woman raised cows and delivered fresh milk to the neighborhood daily. Mother used to pour the fresh milk into a pot and when it began to boil, she removed it from the heat. This was an important step to pasteurize the milk before drinking. When the milk cooled, she placed it in the refrigerator. In the morning, she would reheat the pot of milk to drink with our tea for breakfast. Tea with hot milk is usually served for breakfast in Iraq but we do not drink glasses of milk during the day.

To make tea with milk: Bring ½ cup milk to a boil. Pour the milk into a teacup and add ½ cup hot tea and 1 teaspoon sugar.

Variation: Sometimes to make tea with milk I pour 1 tablespoon of sweetened condensed milk into a cup and then pour in ½ cup of tea from the teapot and ½ cup of boiling water from the kettle and stir. I treat myself with this tea in the afternoon and I am sure your children will enjoy it, too.

CHAMOMILE TEA CHAI BAYBOUN

This tea has a soothing quality and is served to people who are sick or have a cold.

Bring 4 cups of water to a boil. Add ½ cup dried chamomile flowers and leaves. Boil for 15 minutes. Remove from heat and cover to steep for 10 minutes. Pour into cups and sweeten with honey or sugar.

DRIED LIME TEA CHAI NOOMI BASRA / CHAI HAMUTH

You can find whole dried lime or crushed dried lime in Middle Eastern stores. This tea is also used for medicinal purposes. It is prescribed for someone who has an upset stomach or loose stools.

Crush 5 dried limes and remove the seeds. Place in a pot and add 4 cups of water. Bring to a boil and boil for 20 minutes. Pour in tea demitasse cups (*istikans*) and add sugar to taste.

HOMEMADE WINE
NABEETH / SHARAB

Wine making is very common in Mosul and the northern villages in Iraq. Wine was consumed in ancient Mesopotamia, and wine recipes were discovered on clay tablets. Wine was available in ancient Assyria in the north. About two thousands liters of wine were stored in special vessels at Nimrud palace between 791 and 779 BC. Wine was made once a year, when the grapes ripened in the foothills of the mountains in the north. During Nebuchadnezzar's time, wine was called "mountain beer." There are records showing women ran wine shops in 1800 BC. It was a luxury item served only to the gods and the wealthy. Many wines were named after their places of origin.

DATE WINE

SHARAB IL TAMIR

While visiting my sister Samar, I was served her homemade wine. It was very clear and smooth and did not give me a wine headache. She shared her recipe with me, using ingredients from her kitchen shelf. This is a natural method, no chemicals or additives used.

Ingredients

2 pounds dates

4 pounds sugar

27 cups water

4 teaspoons baker's yeast or wine
   yeast

2 teaspoons citric acid

1 cup white wine

3 slices lemon

½ apple, sliced

Note: You will need a large glass jar, about 8 to10 quarts, or two smaller ones. It is important to sanitize the jar and all equipment and work surfaces before you start. You can use a plastic food storage container, but I prefer to use a glass jar for the fermentation process.

Preparation

Combine all the ingredients in an 8- to 10-quart sterilized jar and stir well until the sugar has dissolved. Cover the top of the jar with a plastic bag and secure it with a rubberband. Set aside.

You should see the foaming and fermenting activity within 24 hours. Stir the mixture every day for 5 days until the fermentation activity has stopped.

Remove the dates from the wine mixture and discard. Seal the top of the jar and place it in a dark place at a temperature between 70 and 78 degrees F. Leave the mixture undisturbed for 40 days. You will notice the solids settling in the bottom of the jar.

Siphon the wine to another jar using a plastic tube, making sure to leave the sediments behind. If the wine is cloudy, leave it for a few days to settle, and siphon it again to another jar to further remove the solids from the wine. Seal the jar and leave it to age for a few months. It will taste like sherry after 2 years.

FRUIT SYRUP DRINK

SHARBAT

Sharbat is fruit syrup that we prepare from fresh fruit juices. Many flavors of sharbat are served for guests during the summer and we prepare orange syrup during winter when oranges are in season, and a variety of sharbats are sold by street vendors year around. You can use this recipe to make many different fruit syrups, using berry, plum, pomegranate, sour orange (narinj), and grape juices but orange juice is most popular.

Ingredients

4 cups fresh fruit juice

6 cups granulated sugar

½ cup lemon juice

Preparation

Mix fruit juice of choice with sugar in a large pot. Simmer on low heat for 1 hour, stirring occasionally and removing any scum that develops on top.

Add lemon juice and simmer for an additional 30 minutes. Remove from heat and cool overnight.

Pour fruit syrup into bottles and seal tightly. Store bottles in the refrigerator for up to 6 months.

To serve, pour ¼ cup of fruit syrup into a tall glass. Add ice and cold water to fill the glass. Stir and serve to guests. It is very refreshing!

BREAKFAST, JAMS
&
OMELETS

Breakfast

Breakfast is an important meal of the day that our bodies need when we get up in the morning. In Iraq egg dishes, such as half-boiled eggs, fried eggs and omelets, are very common but cereals are not. Breads, such as *kubuz*, a flat bread, and *sammoun*, an oval fish-shaped bread, are a staple served with clotted cream made from buffalo milk (*qeemar*), date syrup (*dibis*), honey, jams, and butter. Other items on the breakfast menu are tahini and date syrup, yogurt and cheese, olives, tomatoes, and cucumbers. Hot tea is served and sometimes hot milk is added to it. Fruit juices are available as well as strong black coffee.

Broad beans (*tashreeb bajilla*) are popular as a breakfast dish and as a snack from street vendors. Broad beans are soaked overnight and boiled for an hour until tender. Salt is added last and dried water mint (*butnij*) is sprinkled over them. They are always served in a soup bowl over torn pieces of bread and sometimes topped with fried egg, chopped tomatoes, and scallions.

Breakfast during Ramadan, called *suhur*, consists of fruit, grains, puddings, and leftovers from the dinner meal. It must be eaten before dawn and serve as nourishment until the next meal after 16 hours of fasting from sunrise to sunset.

Kahi is pastry similar to puff pastry made of flour, salt, and water. Using a thin rolling pin (*shobak*), the dough is rolled out very thin, buttered, and folded a few times into squares. The dough is then arranged on trays and placed on a bed of ice to keep the butter firm until it is baked at 400 degrees F. Honey or syrup with rose water is drizzled over it as soon as it comes out of the oven. It is also served with *qeemar* cream and date syrup (*dibis*). *Kahi* bakeries are most popular and crowded during the month of Ramadan and during the Muslim feasts. We always treated ourselves with *kahi* and *qeemar* on Fridays which is the weekend in Iraq.

YOGURT LABAN

When I was a child growing up in Baghdad, we would have relatives visiting from Mosul. They would bring a very big sack (like a pillow with a string) of sheep milk yogurt. We put the sack in a big aluminum bowl to catch the whey draining from the yogurt. The longer the yogurt stayed in the bowl, the thicker it became. We used to eat it with bread or make shinina drink: Put 3 tablespoons of drained yogurt in a glass and add a little salt and some water and ice and stir. We used to mix it in a water jug and pour it in glasses just like a buttermilk drink. We drank it with our lunch, which was the biggest meal of the day. This is also a very common drink sold by street vendors.

To make yogurt, bring 1 gallon of milk to a boil. Remove from heat and when it has cooled, but is still warm, stir in 2 tablespoons of yogurt. Cover the pot with towels and put in a warm place in the kitchen. Allow to sit for about 6 hours until the yogurt is set. Then store in the refrigerator.

Notes:
Yogurt becomes very sour when you leave it longer on the kitchen counter. If yogurt does not set properly, place the bowl of yogurt in a pan of hot water for at least 3 hours to activate the fermentation process.

These days, people add a few tablespoons of powdered milk to thicken the commercial milk sold in stores. Sheep's milk is the best tasting milk for making yogurt or cheese, but is not available in the big cities. We used the fresh cow's milk that was delivered to us daily. People now buy commercial milk in stores to make yogurt, but it is not as tasty as the fresh milk.

ARABIC CHEESE JIBIN

Sheep and goats outnumber cattle in Iraq, and sheep's and goat's milk cheeses are more common than those made from cow's milk. Buffalo's milk and cheeses are also very popular in the middle and southern regions of the country.

Cheeses produced locally include white plain Arabic cheese, garlic cheese, herb cheese, braided Armenian stringy cheese, and *beiza* Kurdish cheese. These cheeses are usually preserved in saltwater and kept in large glass jars or pottery urns called *bastooga*. Before serving the cheese, we slice it and leave it in a bowl of fresh water for at least 10 minutes to drain out the salt. Imported cheeses are available, but white Arabic cheese is a staple. Bedouins eat dates with cheese and bread. When there is no cheese, they eat plain yogurt with dates and bread.

Arabic and feta cheeses, accompanied with mint, cucumbers, and tomatoes, are served for breakfast or with tea after the afternoon nap, usually after 4:00 p.m. Arabic cheese can also be served with watermelon and cantaloupe.

CREAM

QEEMAR

8 servings

Buffalo's milk is used for this recipe, but you can substitute heavy cream from cow's milk. In the Iraqi countryside, this dish is enjoyed from a communal tray. Bread is dipped in both date syrup and cream (qeemar wa dibis) with fingers used as utensils. Some Iraqis prefer honey with qeemar especially in the Kurdish areas of the north.

Ingredients

- 1 teaspoon cornstarch
- 1 gallon fresh buffalo's milk (high fat content)

Preparation

Mix cornstarch with milk in a large pot. Put on low heat until the cream rises to the surface and begins to boil. Remove from heat. When it cools, place in refrigerator, covered, for 6 hours.

Skim off the thick layer of cream that has formed on the top of the milk and put the cream on a plate. Cover and refrigerate. Serve with honey or date syrup (*dibis*). (Use the rest of the milk for drinking or making yogurt.)

Every summer, I make a special trip to the Middle Eastern grocery store looking for fresh dates on the stem. They usually are available in the market in mid-August. They are crunchy and not too sweet. When I keep them on the kitchen counter for a few days, the dates ripen and change color to a light brown and become very sweet. Sometimes I freeze a bag of them for use in the winter. These yellow dates turn light brown when I freeze them and they taste like candy!

DATE SYRUP

DIBIS / SILAN

There are 531 different species of dates produced in Iraq. The total of annual production is 350,000 tons of this fruit which makes it a major industry and export. Date syrup is canned and can be purchased commercially. When I was unable to find the syrup locally, I was able to make it myself and use it for breakfast and for baking. Dibis is added to sesame paste (tahini) and spread on bread just like peanut butter and jam. We eat it for breakfast or with tea in the afternoon. During Lent, the tahini and dibis mixture is a popular snack with bread. For this recipe use very soft and ripe dates such as majdool dates or baking dates.

Ingredients

3 cups ripe dates
6 cups water

Preparation

In a large pot, cook the dates in the water on low heat, stirring so they do not stick to the bottom of the pan. When the dates get very soft, pour the mixture through cheesecloth in a bowl to drain the juice. Discard the dates.

Put the date juice back in the pot and cook over very low heat for a few hours, uncovered, removing the scum that develops on top of the juice.

After 2 to 3 hours most of the water will have evaporated and what is left is the syrup. Leave it to cool for a few hours. Then put it in sterilized jars and seal them. Use within 6 months.

APRICOT JAM
MURABA MISHMISH

Ripe soft apricots, which are sweeter and more flavorful, are best suited for making jam. I like to serve this jam as a topping for vanilla ice cream.

Ingredients

3 pounds apricots

3 cups sugar

5 cardamom pods

2 tablespoons lemon juice

Variations: You can use this recipe to make peach and plum jams also.

Preparation

Wash the apricots and remove pits. Keep them whole or chop them. (I prefer to keep them whole.)

Layer the sugar and apricots in a large pot. Add ½ cup of water and the cardamom pods. Simmer uncovered for 1 hour or until the apricots are cooked, skimming off the scum on top as it forms.

Add lemon juice and cook for 20 more minutes. Remove from heat and set aside to cool. Pour into sterilized jars and store in refrigerator.

FIG JAM
MURABA TIN

Every year in mid-August, I make a few jars of fig jam. I usually visit my friends who have a large fig tree and they invite me to pick the figs from their tree. The figs are large and plump. Some of them are very ripe and some are still green and hard. You have to know which ones to pick. While I was sampling these luscious figs and picking them from the tree, I noticed many of them were sampled by the birds and insects. I had a nice full basket to take home, but left a lot for the birds. You can chop the figs, but I prefer to keep them whole when I cook them.

Ingredients

3 pounds fresh figs (red or yellow)

5 cups sugar

8 cardamom pods

¼ cup fresh lemon juice

Preparation

Wash the figs and put in a colander to drain.

Put a layer of sugar in a pot and top it with a layer of figs. Keep layering and then put the cardamom pods on top. Put the pot on the stove on medium heat. When it starts to boil, skim the scum that develops on top. Lower the heat and simmer the figs for 1 hour, uncovered. Make sure to check them and stir them a few times.

Add the lemon juice and leave them to simmer for 20 more minutes, uncovered, or until the syrup thickens. Turn off the heat and leave them to cool. Pour into sterilized jars and keep in the refrigerator for up to 3 months.

CANDIED POMELO PEEL
MURABA TRINGE MARMALADE

This is a very special jam that we serve with Arabic coffee instead of a piece of candy. To serve them to guests, we slice the skins into 1-inch strips and roll each piece in flaked coconut and arrange on a plate.

Ingredients

2 large California pomelos

1 teaspoon salt

4 cups sugar

⅓ cup lemon juice

6 whole cardamom pods or
   1 cinnamon stick

 4 whole cloves

Preparation

Using a sharp paring knife, cut each pomelo in half. Remove the pulp and save it for juicing. Cut the peel with the white pith in five sections or slice it into wide strips.

Place the peel in a bowl of water and leave to soak for 2 hours; then discard the water. Repeat the process four times. This will remove the bitter flavor of the peel.

Put the peel in a large pot. Pour in 8 cups of boiling water and add salt. Bring to a boil and cook for 30 minutes, uncovered. Pour into a colander to drain (discard the water) and cool the peel for 20 minutes. Squeeze all the water out of the pomelo peel.

In a deep pot, combine 1 cup of water, the sugar, lemon juice, and spices, and bring to a boil. Add the pomelo peel and simmer gently for 1 hour or until the skins turn transparent and most of the water is absorbed. Remove from the heat and leave to cool. Put in sterilized jars and store in the refrigerator for up to a year.

ORANGE MARMALADE

MURABA BURTUQAL

For this jam, you need to purchase oranges with a thick peel. We usually make it during the winter, when oranges are abundant in the market.

Ingredients

4 large oranges

3 cups sugar

1 cup orange juice

4 whole cardamom pods

4 whole cloves (optional)

Juice of 1 lemon

Preparation

Peel the oranges and slice the peel from each orange into 5 sections. Drop the peels into a bowl of water to cover and soak for 2 hours. Drain and discard water. Repeat the process two more times.

Fill a large pot with water and bring to a boil. Drop the orange peel into the boiling water and cook for 30 minutes. Pour mixture into a colander to drain (discard water). When cool, squeeze all the water out of the peels.

In the meantime, put the sugar, orange juice, 1 cup of water, and spices in a pot and bring to a boil. Add the orange peel and simmer for 45 minutes. Add the lemon juice and simmer for 20 more minutes, uncovered, until the orange peels look transparent and have absorbed some of the syrup.

Remove from heat and pack the peels in a sterilized jar. Pour the syrup over them and seal the jar. Store in the refrigerator for up to 6 months.

FETA CHEESE OMELET

BEYTH BIL JIBIN

2 servings

This is a favorite recipe that my mother used to make for a light dinner or brunch.

Ingredients

4 eggs

½ teaspoon salt

¼ teaspoon Arabian Spice (page 22)

1 tablespoon vegetable oil

½ cup crumbled feta cheese

2 tablespoons chopped Italian parsley

2 tablespoons chopped fresh mint or
   ½ teaspoon dried mint

Tomato slices for decoration

Preparation

Whisk the eggs and add the salt and spice blend.

Heat the oil in a nonstick pan over medium heat and pour in the eggs. Leave the eggs to set in the pan for 3 minutes.

Sprinkle the feta cheese evenly over the omelet and cover the pan for 2 minutes. Uncover and sprinkle the parsley and mint on top. Slide the omelet to a flat plate and decorate the dish with slices of fresh tomatoes.

EGGS WITH DATES

TAMRIYA

1 serving

This is a very delicious omelet that my mother used to make. Sometimes she drizzled date syrup (dibis, page 67) over it too.

Ingredients

5 soft majdool dates

3 eggs

½ teaspoon salt

1 tablespoon butter

Preparation

Cut the dates in half and remove the stones. Whisk the eggs in a bowl and add salt.

Put the butter in a pan and sauté the dates. Pour the eggs on top of the dates and cover the pan for 3 to 5 minutes until the eggs are set. Serve with bread.

GROUND BEEF OMELET

MAKHLAMA

3 servings

Serve this omelet as a light dinner or a brunch. You could also use ground lamb in this recipe.

Ingredients

3 tablespoons vegetable oil

1 onion, chopped

1 pound ground chuck

1 teaspoon salt

1 teaspoon Arabian Spice (page 22)

1 large tomato, chopped

3 eggs

Preparation

In a large nonstick skillet, heat oil and sauté onion. Add the ground chuck and season with salt and spice blend. Cook for 10 minutes.

Add the tomato. Stir and cook for 5 minutes. Crack the eggs and drop onto the mixture in the pan. Cover the pan and leave to cook for 3 minutes or until eggs are set. Serve with bread or on top of toast or in pita bread.

SAUSAGE

BASTURMA

6 servings / 1 sausage

For this recipe, you need to order beef casings from the butcher shop. They are about 3 inches wide and 12 inches long.

Ingredients

2 pounds (20% fat) ground lamb

1 pound (20% fat) ground chuck

6 cloves garlic, crushed

1 tablespoon salt

1 tablespoon ground cumin

1 tablespoon Arabian Spice (page 22)

Beef casing from the butcher

  (*sandaweelat*)

Variation: You can use a shortcut for this recipe. Put the *basturma* filling in a freezer bag instead of the casings and freeze it. When ready to use, take out the meat from the freezer and slice it. Sauté in oil on both side for 5 minutes and add the eggs to it. Cover the pan for 2 minutes until the eggs are set.

Preparation

Mix the meats, garlic, salt, cumin, and spice blend in a bowl. Cover the bowl and leave in the refrigerator for 2 days for the spices to blend well.

Wash the casing to remove the salt and drain well. Stuff the casing with the meat mixture and tie the ends. Prick the casing with a needle to force the air bubbles out. Place the sausage on a table and cover it with a heavy board to press it flat for 6 hours.

Hang the sausage on a line in a cool (about 35 degrees F) ventilated place. After a week or two, the sausage will be ready to eat.

To cook the sausage, you need to peel off the casing and slice the *basturma* into very thin slices. In a pan, sauté the sausage in oil for 2 minutes on each side. Add whole eggs or beaten eggs and cook, covered, until set. You can also serve cooked slices of this sausage as an appetizer.

Red Lentil Soup

SOUPS

Soups

Iraqi soups (*shourba*) are hearty and make substantial meals. They are made with either lamb or chicken combined with a seasonal vegetable or grain, typically in a clear or tomato-based broth. Legume soups are more common in the Kurdish areas of the north, while hearty, thick vegetable stews with lamb are more common in the middle and southern regions. Soup dishes vary a little from one region to another. Dried lime or sour orange juice (*narinj*) is often added to soups and stews.

During Ramadan, Muslims break their fast with comforting soups, and during the holy month of Muharram, meat and split pea soup becomes an important feature in family and neighborhood gatherings, as well as after prayer meetings. Chicken and rice soups are always prepared during sickness. Restaurants serving *pacha* soup which is made of sheep's head, feet, and tripe are open 24 hours to satisfy the craving of customers for an early breakfast meal or late evening meal. I have tried to include most popular soups here as well as some regional specialties.

Narinj are sour mandarin oranges, also called Seville oranges. This fruit made its way to the Mediterranean after the Arab conquest of Spain between 711 and 718 A.D, and the Spaniards called it *naranja*. They have a distinct sour juice which Iraqis use to flavor soups and stews. We also use the juice to make *narinj* syrup, which is served diluted with water as a refreshing beverage during the summer (page 59). We also make jams and marmalades using the skin and some of the juice during winter when this fruit is in season. I also like to use it as a marinade for meat dishes. You can sometimes find *naranja* juice in the Goya food section of grocery stores.

LAMB AND PEARL BARLEY SOUP

HARRISA

This soup, cooked to the consistency of porridge, is very nutritious. In the city of Mosul people like to put all the ingredients for this recipe in a pottery jar and place the jar in a hot tannour oven to cook slowly overnight. They then have a hearty soup when they get up in the morning. This soup brings the family together in the kitchen. The Muslim communities cook this meal during the holy month of Muharram and distribute dishes of it to their neighbors to commemorate the death of Imam Al Hussein.

Ingredients

1 pound pearl barley

2 pounds lamb with bones

1 teaspoon salt

1 teaspoon ground cumin plus more
  for garnish

1 teaspoon Arabian Spice (page 22)

¼ cup butter (optional)

Variations: You can substitute beef for the lamb in this soup.

Preparation

Wash barley and place in a big pot with the lamb with bones and 8 cups of water. Bring to a boil and then reduce the heat and simmer for 2 hour, removing the scum that develops on top and stirring the soup a few times to prevent sticking to the bottom of the pot.

When meat is well cooked and becomes stringy and the barley becomes thick, add the salt, cumin, and spice blend and cook for 30 more minutes, adding more water and salt if needed.

Add butter to pot if using. Sprinkle some ground cumin on top when soup is served.

BARLEY KISHIK SOUP

SHOURBAT KISHIK

6 servings

This is a favorite family recipe that has been passed down through generations. We make sure to cook it during winter when the Swiss chard is abundant. It is a very nutritious and filling soup. The barley juice will thicken the soup and add a sour flavor to it. I like to serve Kibbi Mosul (page 155) with this soup.

Ingredients

3 pounds lamb shanks

1 tablespoon kosher salt

Fermented turnip cubes (from recipe for
    Fermented Barley Juice on page 83)

1 large eggplant, cut in cubes

2 pounds Swiss chard leaves and stalks

1 head garlic, peeled and crushed

3 tablespoons dried mint

4 cups fermented barley juice (page 83)

Lemon juice (optional)

Preparation

In a large pot, bring the lamb shanks to a boil in 6 cups of water and simmer for 90 minutes, until meat is tender. Remove the shanks and set aside to serve later.

Add the salt, turnips, eggplant, and Swiss chard stalks to the pot and cook until vegetables are tender.

Put the Swiss chard greens through a meat grinder or food processor to extract the green juice. Add the green juice, garlic, mint, and barley juice to the pot. Add a little lemon juice if the fermented barley juice does not add enough sour taste. Simmer for 40 minutes. The soup will have a dark green color.

Serve the soup in bowls along with a lamb shank and a few turnips for each person. Serve bread on the side.

FERMENTED BARLEY JUICE KISHIK

This is an ancient recipe from city of Mosul in northern Iraq. We prepare the juice during winter and freeze some to use throughout the rest of the year. This juice, along with the turnips, is used in Barley Kishik Soup on opposite page.

Ingredients

2 pounds pearl barley (*habbiya*)

1 teaspoon salt

1 pound turnip greens, chopped

3 pounds turnips, cut in cubes

1 teaspoon yeast

3 tablespoons dried mint or ½ cup
   chopped fresh mint

Preparation

Boil the barley in 10 cups of water mixed with the salt until soft, about 45 minutes. When cooked, drain the water off (discard water) and place barley into a big jar or a plastic container.

Add the turnip greens, turnips, yeast, and mint to the jar. Mix well, cover with a towel, and keep in a warm place for 9 days. Stir the mixture after 2 days; then stir the mixture every day to complete the fermentation process.

At this stage, remove the turnip cubes and reserve them in a bowl (they will be used in the Barley Kishik Soup or you can freeze them for use later). Run the barley mixture through a grinder and then put in a strainer and extract the juice. Discard the barley and solids.

You can either freeze the juice until ready to use or use right away in the recipe for Barley Kishik Soup (opposite page).

LAMB SHANK SOUP

TASHRIB LAHAM GHANAM

4 servings

This soup is a family favorite. It is very satisfying on a cold winter's day. We serve it as a meal by itself with toasted bread on the side. I use a pressure cooker to save time when making this soup, otherwise it takes 90 minutes for the shanks to cook on top of the stove.

Ingredients

4 lamb shanks

2 large onions, sliced

½ pound dried chickpeas, soaked in water overnight

1 teaspoon salt

½ teaspoon Arabian Spice (page 22)

Dried or toasted bread slices

Variations: You can also add 3 tablespoons tomato paste to the soup if you prefer.

You could use canned chickpeas and add them to the shanks when cooked.

Sometimes we add 1 tablespoon of crushed dried lime (*noomi basra*) to the soup towards the end.

Preparation

Rinse the shanks and place in a pressure cooker. Add 7 cups of water, onion slices, and chickpeas. Cook for 40 minutes.

Open the cooker and add salt and spice blend and simmer for 10 more minutes or until the meat is cooked.

You can serve each lamb shank in a bowl with the soup, or you can remove the meat from the bones and serve the meat with chickpeas in a bowl over a few pieces of dried bread.

CHICKEN SOUP WITH DRIED LIME

TASHRIB DIJAJ BIL NOOMI BASRA

6 to 8 servings

This hearty soup is traditionally served in the southern provinces of Iraq, such as Basra, Diwaniya, and Nasiriya. The ingredients may vary slightly from region to region, but it always warms you up during cold winter months.

Ingredients

1 3-pound whole chicken, cut up

1 large onion, sliced

1 cinnamon stick

1 teaspoon salt

1 teaspoon Arabian Spice (page 22)

2 or 3 whole dried limes (*noomi Basra*), plus ½ cup crushed dried limes

2 tablespoons butter

Tannour bread for serving

Sliced radishes, sliced onions, and parsley for serving

Preparation

Wash the chicken and place in a deep pot. Sauté on both sides until brown. Add the onion and cinnamon stick and season with salt and the spice blend. Cook for 10 minutes. Add 8 cups of water and bring to a boil.

Crush the whole dried limes and remove the seeds as they give a bitter flavor. Add the limes to the chicken. Lower heat, cover, and simmer for 45 minutes, until chicken pieces are cooked.

Remove chicken from soup and place in a bowl to cool. When cooled, remove the skin and bones. Sauté the chicken pieces in butter and set aside.

Check the soup in the pot to see if it needs more salt or spices. You could also add more water if needed. To serve this dish, put pieces of bread in the bottom of the soup bowls. Sprinkle 1 tablespoon of crushed dried lime over the bread. Ladle the soup over the bread and top with chicken pieces. Serve with sliced radishes, sliced onions, and parsley.

CHICKEN SOUP WITH CHICKPEAS

SHOURBAT DIJAJ BIL HUMMUS

4 to 6 servings

If you use dried chickpeas instead of canned, make sure to soak them in water overnight. Cook them with the chicken but don't add the salt until the cooking is done or the chickpeas might not cook properly.

Ingredients

3 tablespoons vegetable oil

1 3-pound whole chicken

1 large onion, sliced

3 cloves garlic, sliced

1 teaspoon salt

1 teaspoon Arabian Spice (page 22)

4 whole cardamom pods

½ teaspoon ground cumin

½ teaspoon ground coriander

1 (16-ounce) can tomato sauce

1 (15-ounce) can chickpeas, rinsed
   and drained

Juice of 1 lemon

Chopped parsley for decoration

Preparation

Heat the vegetable oil in a deep pot and sauté the chicken for 5 minutes on each side to brown. Add the onion, garlic, salt, and spices. Allow them to cook in the oil for 5 minutes. Add the tomato sauce and simmer for 5 more minutes. Pour 6 cups of water over the chicken and bring to a boil. Cover and simmer for 35 minutes, until the chicken is cooked.

Add the chickpeas and lemon juice and cook for 15 more minutes. Remove the chicken from the soup and debone it. Return the chicken meat to the pot and turn off the heat. Ladle the soup into soup bowls and decorate each with 1 tablespoon of chopped parsley. Serve with *saj* or *tannour* bread.

CHICKEN SOUP WITH RICE

SHOURBAT DIJAJ

4 servings

This is a hearty soup to serve for lunch or dinner as a whole meal. It is rather thick and is a comforting favorite during sickness or cold weather. You could add tomato sauce to the broth if you like. You could also cook this soup with noodles (rishta) instead of rice. Sometimes, I add a few cardamom pods to the pot while the chicken is cooking to add a delicious flavor.

Ingredients

1 chicken, cut up

1 teaspoon salt

½ cup white rice

Preparation

Put the cut-up chicken in a pot. Add 5 cups of water and salt. Bring to a boil and remove the scum that rises to top. Simmer chicken for 30 minutes. Add rice and simmer, half covered, for an additional 40 minutes, until chicken is cooked and rice grains are very soft. Remove chicken skins and/or bones before serving, if desired.

Note: This soup thickens as it cools, you can add ½ cup of water when reheating it if needed.

BARLEY AND LENTIL SOUP
BURMA

This soup is a wonderful treat on a cold winter's day. It is a full meal by itself when served with bread on the side. Use pearl barley which is processed and polished to remove the bran. This soup tends to thicken when it cools. You can always add more water when reheating it.

Ingredients

1 cup pearl barley

½ cup dry chickpeas, soaked overnight in water

1 cup brown lentils

1 cup chopped onions

¼ cup olive oil

1 teaspoon salt

1 teaspoon ground cumin

Preparation

Wash barley, chickpeas, and lentils and drain. Place them in a big pot with 8 cups of water and bring to a boil. Lower the heat and simmer for 1 hour, keeping the pot half covered and stirring from time to time to keep them from sticking to the bottom of the pot.

Sauté onions in oil and add salt and ground cumin. Pour over the soup and stir. Taste and add more salt if needed.

BROWN LENTIL SOUP

SHOURBAT ADAS ASMAR

4 servings

This is a comforting winter soup, and can serve as a complete meal with toasted bread on the side. This soup tends to thicken as it cools. You can always add more water when reheating it.

Ingredients

12 ounces brown lentils

1 pound stewing beef or lamb, cut in
   1-inch cubes

1 large onion, chopped

2 tablespoons olive oil or butter

1 teaspoon kosher salt

1 teaspoon ground cumin

½ teaspoon Arabian Spice (page 22)

Bread for serving

Preparation

Wash the lentils, drain them, and put in a deep pot. Wash meat and add to pot. Add 6 cups of water and bring to a boil. Skim off the scum that develops on top.

Simmer for 1 hour on medium heat with the lid half open, stirring a few times to keep the lentils from sticking to the bottom of the pot.

In a skillet, sauté the onion in olive oil, and add salt, cumin, and spice blend. When onions are soft and translucent add to the soup and simmer for 20 minutes. Taste and add more salt and spices as needed. Serve with bread.

BULGUR AND LENTIL SOUP

MUJADARA MASLAWIYA

This is a vegetarian soup we prepared during Lent. It originated in Mosul, a city in north Iraq. My mother is from Mosul and we grew up to enjoy many grain dishes. This soup is served as a whole meal. It tends to become thick when it cools off but you can always add more water when reheating it.

Ingredients

1 cup lentils

½ cup medium bulgur

½ cup toasted noodles (*rishta*), or
    egg noodles

1 teaspoon salt

1 teaspoon Arabian Spice (page 22)

1 medium onion, chopped

¼ cup olive oil

Preparation

Bring 6 cups of water to a boil in a large pot. Rinse lentils and bulgur and add to the boiling water. Cook for 35 minutes.

If using egg noodles, saute noodles in a little oil until toasted. Add noodles, salt, and spice blend to the soup. Cook for 10 more minutes, stirring a few times to prevent the bulgur from sticking to the bottom of the pot.

In a skillet, sauté onions in oil until soft and lightly brown. Add to the soup and simmer on low heat, covered, for 15 minutes. Serve with toasted bread.

RED LENTIL SOUP

SHOURBAT ADAS

4 servings

When you cook red lentils they turn yellow in color. Legume soups are very popular in winter, especially in northern Iraq. When I cook this hearty soup, I remember my mother making it whenever she cooked grilled lamb kababs.

Ingredients

1 cup red lentils

½ cup whole grain rice

6 cups water or chicken broth

1 large onion, chopped

4 tablespoons butter

½ tablespoon curry powder

½ tablespoon ground cumin

1 teaspoon salt

Ground cumin and lemon halves for
   decoration

Preparation

Rinse lentils and rice and put in a pot. Add the water or broth and boil for 40 minutes with the lid half open.

In a skillet, sauté onion in butter and then add curry powder, cumin, and salt. When the onions are tender, add to the soup and stir well. Simmer on low heat for 10 more minutes.

Sprinkle cumin on top before serving. You can also squeeze the juice of half a lemon on top of each serving if you prefer.

PURSLANE SOUP

SHOURBAT BERBEEN

Purslane is an edible weed that is very hard to find in American grocery stores. I usually find it at farmers markets. If you have this edible weed growing during the summer in your yard, you can make this very delicious slightly sour soup. Make sure to harvest it before the flower buds open, using the leaves and stems to make the soup.

Ingredients

1 medium onion, chopped

3 tablespoons vegetable oil

1 teaspoon salt

½ teaspoon Arabian Spice (page 22)

1 large tomato, chopped

1 tablespoon tomato paste

2 cups chopped purslane

2 cups water or stock

Preparation

In a large pot, sauté onion in vegetable oil for a few minutes. Add salt and spice blend and stir.

Add tomato, tomato paste, and purslane and stir. Add water or stock, cover the pot, and bring to a boil. Reduce the heat, and simmer for 15 minutes. Serve with toasted bread.

SWISS CHARD SOUP

SHOURBAT SILIQ

4 servings

This is a winter soup that we cook when Swiss chard is abundant in the market. We use both the leaves and the stalks for this recipe. You could substitute fresh or frozen spinach for the Swiss chard if you prefer. It is a simple and healthful soup to make for your family.

Ingredients

1 medium onion, chopped

4 large cloves garlic, crushed

3 tablespoons olive oil

1 teaspoon salt

1 teaspoon Arabian Spice (page 22)

5 cups water or broth

½ cup rice

1 bunch Swiss chard, washed
    and chopped

⅓ cup lemon juice

1 teaspoon dried mint

Toasted bread for serving

Preparation

In a skillet, sauté the onion and garlic in oil for 3 minutes. Add salt, spice blend, and water or broth. When it starts to boil, add the rice. Simmer for 20 minutes.

Add Swiss chard, lemon juice, and mint. Simmer until Swiss chard is cooked, about 10 more minutes. Serve with toasted bread.

FAVA BEAN SOUP

TASHRIB BAJILLA

This soup is a very popular street food in Iraq that you can eat for breakfast or any time of the day. It is high in protein and low in fat and an economic meal for low income village populations. For this recipe, you can use canned fava beans, but traditionally we use dried fava beans and soak them overnight in water. Make sure to add salt after the beans are fully cooked otherwise they will harden and not properly cook if you add salt in the beginning. We use dried water mint in this recipe. It has a distinct flavor. If you are unable to find it, you could use dried oregano as a substitute.

Ingredients

1 pound dry fava beans

1 teaspoon salt

2 teaspoons dried water mint (*butnij*), divided

Toasted *tannour* bread for serving

1 tablespoon butter or olive oil

2 tablespoons fresh lemon juice

Chopped tomatoes and chopped scallions for decoration

Preparation

Wash the fava beans and put them in a bowl of water to soak overnight.

Drain the beans and put them in a deep pot with 6 cups of water. Bring to a boil and simmer over medium heat for 40 minutes, until the beans are soft. Add salt and 1 teaspoon water mint. Simmer for 10 more minutes.

To serve the soup, place a few pieces of *tannour* bread in a large soup bowl and scoop the beans over the bread. Heat the butter or oil in a pan and drizzle it over the fava beans. Top with the lemon juice and sprinkle remaining 1 teaspoon water mint over. Sprinkle with chopped tomatoes and scallions.

PUMPKIN SOUP

SHOURBAT SHIJAR

We usually make this soup during the winter when pumpkins are in season. We also use the soup base for cooking Rice Kibbi (page 147), but it is delicious by itself as a plain light soup.

Ingredients

2 tablespoons olive oil

1 small onion, chopped

2 cloves garlic, sliced

6 cups lamb broth or water

1 tablespoon salt

1 teaspoon Arabian Spice (page 22)

2 cups peeled and chopped pumpkin

Juice of ½ lemon

Preparation

Heat olive oil in a large pot and sauté onion and garlic. Add broth or water, salt, and spice blend and bring to a boil. Add the pumpkin. Cover and simmer for 20 minutes or until the pumpkin is soft.

Add lemon juice and simmer for 10 more minutes.

For a smooth, thick, and creamy texture use an immersion blender to blend the soup in the pot. Simmer for an additional 10 minutes.

Alternatively, for a chunkier soup, just put half of the soup in a blender and purée until smooth. Then return the purée to the rest of the soup in the pot and simmer for 10 minutes.

APRICOT SOUP

SHOURBAT QAISY

This is a hearty, sweet and rich soup that we cook once a year on New Year's Day, supposedly to sweeten the New Year and bring your family luck as well. It is very satisfying on a cold winter's day and keeps for two to three days in the refrigerator.

Ingredients

2 pounds lamb shanks

1 teaspoon salt

1 pound dried apricots

½ cup raisins

½ cup blanched almonds

3 tablespoons sugar, if needed

3 cinnamon sticks

½ teaspoon ground allspice

Preparation

Place the meat in a large pot and add salt and 6 cups of water. Simmer for 90 minutes, until the meat is tender and comes off the bone.

Add the apricots, raisins, almonds, sugar, cinnamon sticks, and allspice and simmer for 20 minutes.

Remove the cinnamon sticks. Remove the meat from the bones and return meat to the pot. Serve in soup bowls with toasted bread.

Variation: You can add 15 to 20 rice *kibbi* (page 147) to this soup and boil them for 20 minutes (add 2 cups of water before dropping the *kibbi* into the sauce). When *kibbi* rises to the top, they are done.

Chickpea Salad

SALADS

Salads

Iraqis serve salads composed of raw, cooked, or pickled vegetables as appetizers or with the meal. We use whatever we find at the market. We are able to find cauliflower, tomatoes, cucumbers, and beets in the grocery stores throughout the year. When in season, a dish of fresh parsley, scallions, and mint is always served with the meal. Pickled turnips, cabbage, cauliflower, and olives are served in a bowl as these foods are believed to stimulate the appetite.

We enjoy fresh tomatoes and cucumbers during the summer. Whole heads of romaine lettuce are eaten as a snack without any dressing. When chopped, we add chopped tomatoes and cucumbers and dress it with homemade vinegar or lemon and olive oil. We do not measure the dressing but pour it just by eye and taste it to check if it needs more lemon or salt.

ARABIC SALAD
SALATA

This salad is very common throughout the Middle East. The Lebanese variation of this recipe adds toasted pita chips and summac. They call it fattoush. *My family loves the earthy, delicious flavors of this salad. My son thinks it tastes even better the next day.*

Ingredients

3 tomatoes, chopped

½ cup chopped scallions

2 cucumbers, peeled and chopped

½ cup fresh Italian parsley, chopped

1 green pepper, chopped

1 teaspoon salt

⅓ cup olive oil

⅓ cup lemon juice

¼ cup apple cider vinegar

Preparation

In a big salad bowl, mix all the chopped vegetables and sprinkle with salt.

In a small bowl, combine olive oil, lemon juice, and vinegar. Pour the dressing on top of vegetables and stir. Cover and refrigerate for 30 minutes before serving.

BEET SALAD

SALATAT SHWANDAR

Beets are a winter root vegetable and I love to make this salad when they are in season. I buy the beets with the green tops attached to ensure sweet flavor and freshness. I usually chop the green tops, sauté them in oil and garlic, add salt and lemon juice at the end and serve it as a side dish. This beet salad will keep in the refrigerator for a week.

Ingredients

3 pounds fresh beets

1 teaspoon salt, divided

⅓ cup apple cider vinegar

2 cloves garlic, sliced

2 tablespoons chopped fresh Italian
    parsley

Preparation

Rinse beets and cut off ends. Place in a pot of water and add ½ teaspoon of salt. Boil for 30 minutes, half covered, on medium heat until beets are tender.

When beets are tender, remove from water and cool. Peel and cut them into slices or cubes and place them in a bowl.

Add vinegar, garlic, and remaining ½ teaspoon of salt to beets and toss. Garnish with chopped parsley. Cover and refrigerate for at least 1 hour for the flavors to blend before serving.

BOILED TURNIPS
SHALGHAM

6 servings

Turnips are a winter vegetable and a very popular snack served by street cart vendors in Iraq. When we cook turnips at home we add beets to produce a beautiful reddish color. We then pour the beet and turnip water into cups and drink it like tea.

Ingredients

3 pounds turnips
1 pound beets
2 tablespoons date syrup (*dibis*, page 67) or sugar
1 teaspoon salt

Preparation

Rinse the turnips and beets and cut the tops and bottoms off. Halve the turnips across the middle, and slice the beets. Place in a pot and cover with a heatproof plate to keep the vegetables submerged.

Pour 6 cups of water in the pot and add the date syrup. Bring to a boil and cook for 10 minutes. Add salt and cook, covered, for 20 more minutes or until vegetables are soft. Drain and serve them in a bowl sprinkled with more salt if you prefer.

CHICKPEA SALAD

SALATA BIL HUMMUS

4 servings

This is a very nutritious salad that we prepare throughout the year. It is filling and makes a meal by itself. We take it to picnics, serve it with other appetizers, and prepare it during Lent. Sometimes, I top it with canned tuna fish to make a light lunch or dinner.

Ingredients

1 (18-ounce) can chickpeas
½ cup diced fresh tomatoes
¼ cup chopped scallions
¼ cup chopped red onions
¼ cup chopped Italian parsley
¼ teaspoon salt
Juice of 1 lemon
2 tablespoons vinegar
2 tablespoons olive oil

Preparation

Pour the contents of the can of chickpeas into a colander. Rinse the chickpeas and drain.

Place the chickpeas in a bowl. Add tomatoes, scallions, onions, parsley, and salt, and toss.

Add the lemon juice, vinegar, and olive oil. Toss the salad and refrigerate for about 30 minutes before serving.

POTATO SALAD

SALATAT BATATA

4 servings

This is a very light salad for picnics and is very popular during Lent. It tastes even better the next day, after the potatoes have a chance to absorb the oil and lemon flavors.

Ingredients

4 medium potatoes

1 teaspoon salt

¼ teaspoon Arabian Spice (page 22)

Juice of 1 lemon

2 tablespoons vinegar

¼ cup olive oil

¼ cup chopped scallions

¼ cup chopped fresh Italian parsley

Olives for decoration

Preparation

In a medium pot, boil the potatoes for 30 minutes. When cooked, drain the water and pour cold water over the potatoes to stop the cooking process. Peel the potatoes while they are still warm. Chop them and place them in a salad bowl.

Sprinkle the potatoes with the salt and spice blend. Combine the lemon juice, vinegar, and olive oil and pour over the potatoes while still warm. Add scallions and parsley and toss. Decorate the salad with olives. Refrigerate for at least 1 hour before serving.

Picnic in Baghdad, 1979

PURSLANE SALAD

SALATAT BERBEEN

Purslane is an edible weed plant that grows in the yard during the summer. The stems and the leaves are thick, crunchy, and succulent, with a lemony flavor. We chop the plant and make delicious salads, stews, and soups.

Ingredients

2 cups coarsely chopped purslane

1 cucumber, peeled and chopped

2 medium tomatoes, diced

½ cup chopped scallions

3 tablespoons olive oil

Juice of 1 lemon

1 teaspoon salt

1 clove garlic, chopped

Preparation

In a bowl, combine the purslane, cucumber, tomatoes, and scallions.

In another bowl, whisk the olive oil and lemon juice, and add salt and garlic. Pour over the salad and stir. Refrigerate for 30 minutes before serving.

CAULIFLOWER SALAD

SALATAT QARNABEET

4 servings

Iraqis do not eat cauliflower raw. It is a winter vegetable and we always boil it and add a dressing. This is a very light and healthful salad that you can keep in the refrigerator for up to a week.

Ingredients

½ head (1 pound) cauliflower
1 teaspoon salt, divided
½ lemon
2 tablespoons olive oil
1 tomato, sliced
⅓ cup chopped scallions

Preparation

Wash the cauliflower and place it in a pot of boiling water and add ½ teaspoon of salt. Bring back to a boil, cover and cook for 10 minutes. Remove cauliflower from pot and place it in a colander to cool.

Chop the cauliflower and place in a bowl. Season with the remaining ½ teaspoon of salt. Squeeze lemon juice over and drizzle with olive oil. Decorate with tomato slices and chopped scallions.

ONION WITH SUMMAC

BASAL BIL SUMMAQ

4 servings

We prepare these onions to serve with Tekka Kabab (page 215), Kufta Kabab (page 212), and in a kabab sandwich. They add a tart flavor to the grilled meat.

Ingredients

2 large onions, sliced
1 teaspoon salt
1 tablespoon ground summac

Preparation

Put onions in a bowl and sprinkle with salt. Let sit for 30 minutes to wilt. Squeeze the water from the onions and drain in a colander. Add the summac and stir. Serve them on a plate with kababs or as a side condiment.

YOGURT CUCUMBER SALAD

SALATA BIL LABAN

4 servings

This is a very refreshing salad served as an appetizer or with rice dishes and kababs. During winter when cucumbers are not in season we sometimes replace the cucumbers with thinly sliced romaine lettuce. Purslane is also a delicious substitute for the cucumbers. We use fresh mint during the summer but replace the fresh mint with one teaspoon of dried mint when needed.

Ingredients

2 cups plain low-fat yogurt

1 cucumber, peeled and chopped

2 cloves garlic, crushed

½ cup chopped fresh parsley

¼ cup chopped fresh mint

1 teaspoon salt

Preparation

Mix all the ingredients in a bowl. Cover the bowl and refrigerate for at least an hour before serving. Serve as an appetizer or side salad.

YOGURT DILL SAUCE
LABAN BIL SHIBINT

If fresh dill isn't available, you can use 1 tablespoon of dried dill instead for this recipe. I always keep dried herbs in my cupboard to use when I need them. But remember that dried herbs have a stronger flavor than the fresh herbs so you do not need to use as much. This sauce is delicious with fresh vegetables as a salad.

Ingredients

2 cups plain yogurt

1 clove garlic, crushed

½ teaspoon salt

½ cup chopped fresh dill

Preparation

Put the yogurt in a bowl. Stir in garlic, salt, and dill. Cover the bowl and refrigerate for 30 minutes for the flavors to blend before serving. Serve this sauce as a dip for fresh vegetables or with rice.

Markets in Iraq

There are still traditional markets in Baghdad such as Al-Shorja, the spice market, and Suq Al-Sarai and Suq Al-Safafier for handmade copper, bronze crafts, and aluminum pots and antiques. And there are many markets that specialize in fabrics for men and women. I used to take a trip with my mother a few times a year to go to The River Street (Al-Nahar Street) market and purchase the fabrics to make new dresses to celebrate the feasts and special occasions. Al-Mutanabi Street, which is named after a famous poet, is filled with bookstores selling new and used books, posters, post-cards, and musical recordings, and printing businesses, too.

But today, many residential areas have their own shops that provide the neighborhood with fabric, food, and household items such as Al-Dora, Al-Karadah, Baghdad Al-Jadidah, Al-Mansour, and Palestine Road in Baghdad. And mini-malls and mega-malls are the new destinations for the public to shop for everything in one spot.

RICE
&
OTHER GRAINS

Rice

In Iraq, rice is served with each meal as a side dish with lamb or beef and vegetable stews. When rice is cooked with meat, it becomes a main dish served with salads and pickles. Iraqis consume a variety of rice grown in the country's south-central region of marshy fields. The most popular medium grain aromatic rice is called *ambar*. Many other non-aromatic varieties are also grown or imported for consumption.

Other Grains

The majority of wheat and barley is cultivated in the northern provinces of Nineveh, Kirkuk, and Arbil, and is harvested in June and July. Wheat is processed in special mills to produce different sizes of bulgur. Sizes three and four are used for making bulgur pilaf. Sizes one and two are used for *kibbi* dishes. I remember when big sacks of wheat were delivered to my mother's family in Mosul. They boiled the wheat in 25-inch-diameter pots. When the wheat was cooked, they strained it and spread it on sheets to dry under the hot sun on the roof (*satih*). When the wheat was completely dry, they took it to the mill to grind. Sometimes women who ran a business of grinding wheat visited neighborhoods with their stone grinders (*jarooshi*), and they spent the whole day grinding the bulgur. Every family in the North took pride in their own bulgur. *Jireesh* is uncooked bulgur that we mix with the regular bulgur to make *Kibbi Mosul*. Bulgur is a staple in the north, where it is cooked as a side dish or with meat. People there make different varieties of *kibbi* dishes. *Kibbi Mosul* originated in that city, and the people of Mosul take a great deal of pride in their culinary skills.

WHITE RICE

TIMMAN / RUZ

4 servings

We usually buy long grain rice that is well-aged such as basmati. Rice is a staple with every meal in Iraq and is delicious served with stews.

Ingredients

¼ cup vegetable oil

2 cups white basmati rice

½ teaspoon salt

Preparation

Pour oil in a pot and place it on the stove over medium heat. Wash the rice and drain it in a colander. Add the rice and salt to the pot and stir for about 3 minutes, until the rice is coated with the oil.

Pour in 4 cups of water making sure the water level is half an inch above the rice level. Partially cover and bring to a boil and cook until water is absorbed. (Water will be completely absorbed when you see holes develop on the surface of the rice.) Reduce the heat and simmer, covered, for 20 more minutes or until rice is tender. Uncover the pot and fluff the rice.

It is not easy to make perfect rice. Sometimes rice becomes gummy, and there are a number of reasons for that. If you do not bring the rice to a boil quickly, the rice will stay in the water longer and become gummy or mushy. Sometimes the rice you buy is not aged and requires less water for cooking—if this is the case you could use ½ cup less water. I purchase rice from Indian and Persian stores to make sure the rice is aged. Sautéing the rice in oil will coat the rice grains and help prevent them from getting sticky. The variety and brand of rice is also important. You might have to try different brands of rice until you are satisfied with the results.

RICE WITH NOODLES

TIMMAN BIL SHAARIYA

4 servings

For this recipe, you need to purchase ready-made egg noodles from the pasta section of the grocery store.

Ingredients

3 tablespoons vegetable oil

½ cup dry thin egg noodles

2 cups white basmati rice, rinsed and drained

1 teaspoon salt

1 cinnamon stick

Preparation

In a pot, heat the oil and sauté noodles until lightly toasted. Add the rice to the noodle mixture with the salt, and sauté for 3 minutes until rice grains are coated.

Add cinnamon stick and 3½ cups of water and bring to a boil. When water is almost absorbed, lower the heat and stir the rice. Leave it to simmer for 20 more minutes, covered, until the rice is tender. Remove cinnamon stick before serving.

SAFFRON RICE

TIMMAN ZAAFARAN

4 servings

I make this rice occasionally when I cook a leg of lamb or lamb shanks. I use Spanish or Iranian saffron and add the threads to the water while the rice is cooking. Saffron is a very expensive ingredient, but it is used sparingly in this recipe and imparts a wonderful flavor. To add more flavor to saffron rice, I like to put some cardamom pods in the water while the rice is boiling. You can also add one tablespoon of rosewater towards the end when all the water is absorbed.

Ingredients

2 cups white basmati rice

⅓ cup vegetable oil

1 teaspoon salt

6 cardamom pods

½ teaspoon Spanish saffron

1 tablespoon rosewater (optional)

Preparation

In a large pot, sauté rice in oil for about 3 minutes to coat, and then add salt and cardamom pods and stir. Add saffron and 3½ cups of water and bring to a boil. When the water is almost absorbed, add the rosewater to the rice, if using, and stir. Reduce heat, cover, and simmer for 20 more minutes. You can top this rice with Almond and Raisin Dressing (page 132).

FAVA BEANS WITH RICE AND DILL

TIMMAN BAGILLA BIL SHBINT

6 to 8 servings

This is a very popular dish cooked in Baghdad and southern cities of the country. It is influenced by the Persian cuisine, since there are thousands of pilgrims who come to Karbala to visit the shrines each year. Many of the restaurants began to cook Iranian dishes to cater to these pilgrims. Intermarriages are very common between Iraqis and Persians in this province. Many of the visiting Persians have families residing in Karbala or other cities in the South.

Ingredients

¼ cup vegetable oil

1 medium onion, chopped

1 pound peeled fresh or frozen fava
  beans

1 cup chopped fresh dill or
  3 tablespoons dried dill

1½ teaspoons salt, divided

½ teaspoon Arabian Spice (page 22)

1½ cups white basmati rice

2 cups cooked and shredded chicken
  or stewed lamb

Preparation

In a large skillet, heat oil. Add the onion and sauté. Add fava beans and dill. Season with ½ teaspoon salt and spice blend and add ½ cup of water. Simmer for 5 minutes.

In a separate pot, boil the rice in 2 cups of water with remaining 1 teaspoon of salt for 10 minutes. Drain the rice and pour over the fava bean mixture. (You can add 2 tablespoons of olive oil at this point if desired.) Stir the rice mixture and simmer on low heat until the rice grains are tender.

Serve rice on a platter topped with the cooked chicken or lamb. Accompany with Yogurt Cucumber Salad (page 114).

Note: Fresh fava bean pods are in the same family as pea and green bean pods. You need to shell the beans from the pod and remove the outer skin of each bean. It is a time-consuming project, and as children we were always involved in it. You can find fresh or frozen fava beans in the Asian or Middle Eastern grocery stores. You could replace the fava beans with peas or lima beans if you prefer.

RED RICE

TIMMAN AHMAR

4 servings

We usually cook this rice with fresh tomato juice. In the summer, we purchase bushels of very ripe tomatoes, squeeze the juice out, and then freeze the juice in freezer bags. If you are not able to get ripe tomatoes, canned tomato sauce is a good substitute in this recipe.

Ingredients

- 2 cups white basmati rice, rinsed and drained
- 3 tablespoons vegetable oil
- 1 teaspoon salt
- ½ teaspoon Arabian Spice (page 22)
- 1 cup tomato sauce or fresh tomato juice
- 3 cups water or lamb broth or chicken broth

Variation: You can add frozen peas while rice is boiling, if you prefer.

Preparation

In a large pot, sauté rice in oil until coated, about 3 minutes. Add salt, spice blend, tomato sauce, and water or broth. Cover, bring to a boil and cook until the water is absorbed. Lower the heat and simmer for 20 more minutes, covered, until the rice is tender. Fluff with a spoon.

RED RICE WITH CHICKEN

TIMMAN BIL DIJAJ

6 servings

This dish is a meal in itself. We serve the rice on a big platter topped with pieces of chicken and always include a side dish of fried eggplant.

Ingredients

1 whole chicken

1 medium onion, chopped

6 cardamom pods

1 teaspoon salt

1 tablespoon Arabian Spice (page 22)

1 cup tomato sauce

2 cups white basmati rice, rinsed and
   drained

Variation: You can use stewing lamb instead of the chicken.

Preparation

In a large pot over medium heat, sear the chicken for 5 minutes on each side. Add the onion, cardamom pods, salt, and spice blend. Pour in the tomato sauce and simmer for 15 minutes.

Add 3 cups of water and bring to a boil. Lower the heat and simmer until the chicken is tender. Remove the chicken from the sauce and set aside.

Add the rice to the sauce and bring to a boil. When the rice has absorbed most of the sauce, reduce the heat to low and simmer, covered, for 20 more minutes.

Bone the chicken and discard bones. Serve the rice on a platter topped with chicken pieces. Serve Arabic Salad (pages 105), fried eggplant (page 167), and pickles with this meal.

EGGPLANT WITH RED RICE

MAQLOUBI

"Maqloubi" means "upside down" in Iraq. This dish consists of lamb or chicken layered with sautéed onions, eggplant, and rice in a Dutch oven. After cooking and then resting for 30 minutes, the pot is flipped on a tray to release it's contents and the dish is served as a main meal "upside down."

Ingredients

1 large eggplant

2 tablespoons salt, divided

½ cup or more vegetable oil

1 large onion, sliced

1 green pepper, sliced

1 pound lamb stew meat, cut in
  1-inch cubes

1 (16-ounce) can tomato sauce

2 tomatoes, sliced

1 tablespoon Arabian Spice (page 22)

2 cups white basmati rice

Variation: For a change you could replace the lamb with chicken.

Preparation

Slice the eggplant, sprinkle with 1 tablespoon of salt, and leave to drain in a colander for a ½ hour.

Dry the eggplant slices. In a skillet, heat the oil and fry the eggplant slices on both sides until lightly browned. Remove to a plate. Sauté the onion and green pepper in the oil until soft and set aside.

Place the lamb in a pot and add 4 cups of water. Bring to a boil and then lower heat and simmer for 45 minutes, until tender. Add the tomato sauce and cook for another 20 minutes.

In a large pot, sauté the tomatoes in 1 teaspoon of oil until soft. Arrange the sautéed onion and green pepper on top. Arrange the eggplant slices on top. Add a layer of lamb using a slotted spoon to drain the sauce. Sprinkle with remaining 1 tablespoon salt and the spice blend. Sprinkle the rice on top and then pour the lamb sauce over the rice.

Cover pot and cook over medium heat for 30 minutes. Check the rice to see if the grains are cooked. Reduce the heat and add a little more water if more time is needed. When rice is tender, remove the pot from heat and let sit for 30 minutes, covered, to allow the layers to set.

To serve, remove the cover from the pot. Put a tray or a platter over the pot and holding the tray and the pot together carefully invert the pot on the tray and lift off the pot. Serve with pickles, salads, and yogurt drink.

RICE WITH MEAT AND CARROTS

TIMMAN BIL JIZAR

6 servings

I usually buy the carrots with the green tops attached to them. They have a wonderful, sweet flavor and are fresher. You could use bagged carrots but they could be weeks or months old. For a shortcut, you can use leftover cooked plain white rice and just add it to the meat and carrot mixture when cooked. Stir and leave to simmer for 15 minutes for the rice to absorb the flavor of the meat and carrots.

Ingredients

Meat and Carrot Mixture:

¼ cup vegetable oil

1 pound ground chuck or lamb

1 large onion, chopped

1 teaspoon salt

1 teaspoon Arabian Spice (page 22)

1 cup peeled and chopped carrots

Rice:

3 tablespoons vegetable oil

1½ cups white basmati rice

1 teaspoon salt

Preparation

Meat and Carrot Mixture:

Heat oil in a pan and sauté the meat for 10 minutes. Add onion, salt, and spice blend and stir. Cook until the onions are soft. Add the carrots and stir the mixture. Pour in ½ cup of water and simmer for 15 minutes, until carrots are tender. Set aside.

Rice:

Pour the oil in a pot. Add rice and salt and sauté for 3 minutes to coat rice with oil. Add 3 cups of water, cover, bring to a boil, and cook until water is almost absorbed.

When water is almost absorbed, add the meat and carrot mixture to the rice and stir. Reduce heat to low and simmer, covered, for 20 minutes or until rice grains are tender. (If you prefer, you could cook the rice all the way through separately and then plate the rice on a platter and top it with the meat and carrot mixture.)

RICE DRESSINGS

You can make a variety of "dressings" to decorate and flavor rice when you have guests. You can prepare these dressings ahead and keep them in the refrigerator for a day or two. When ready to use, reheat the dressing in a sauté pan and spread over rice.

ALMOND AND RAISIN DRESSING FOR RICE
LOUZ AND KISHMISH   4 servings

Ingredients

3 tablespoons vegetable oil

1 cup slivered almonds

½ cup golden raisins

½ teaspoon cinnamon

½ teaspoon allspice

Preparation

Heat oil in a skillet and sauté almonds until toasted. Add raisins and sauté for 1 minute. Sprinkle spices over the mixture and remove from heat. When you serve white rice or saffron rice, spread the dressing on top.

NOODLE DRESSING FOR RICE
SHAARIYA   4 servings

Ingredients

2 tablespoons vegetable oil

1 cup dry thin egg noodles

¾ cup chicken or lamb broth

Preparation

Heat oil in a skillet and sauté noodles until lightly toasted. Add broth and bring to a boil. When all the broth is absorbed, spread the noodles on top of cooked rice.

MEAT DRESSING FOR RICE

TIMMAN BIL QEEMA   **6 to 8 servings**

"Qeema" is ground beef or lamb sautéed with chopped onions and seasoned with salt and Arabian Spice. We serve it with plain rice or mix it with peas and other vegetables to make a stew. We also prepare it as a filling for vegetables and some kibbi dishes and omelets. I prepare qeema ahead of time, spoon it into small containers, and keep it in the freezer for future use.

Ingredients

½ pound ground lamb or beef

2 tablespoons vegetable oil, divided

½ cup chopped onion

½ teaspoon salt

½ teaspoon Arabian Spice (page 22)
   plus more for sprinkling

Preparation

In a nonstick pan sauté meat in 1 tablespoon of oil. When meat is halfway cooked, add the onion, salt, and spice blend, and stir. Keep sautéing until the onions are cooked. Spread this dressing over Saffron Rice (page 123) or white rice and sprinkle with additional Arabian Spice.

RICE IN A CURTAIN

PERDE PLAU

My mother used to make this dish for New Year's Day and other special occasions. Influenced by Turkish cuisine, it is a rice dish baked inside dough and makes a beautiful presentation. Every family has its own recipe for the rice filling. You can add diced lamb or cooked chicken pieces or even meatballs to the rice mixture. I use a spring-form cake pan and line it with the dough. Then pour in the rice filling and cover the rice with the dough and bake it. The recipe is very popular in the Kurdish areas and in Baghdad. It is very involved and takes a few hours to prepare, but is well worth the effort. I usually prepare the dough the day before and keep it in the refrigerator.

Ingredients

Dough (Curtain):

2 cups all-purpose flour, plus more if
   needed

1 teaspoon salt

4 tablespoons vegetable oil, divided

1 teaspoon dry yeast

½ cup warm water

1 teaspoon sugar

(Continued on page 137)

Variation: A modern variation of this recipe uses phyllo dough in the place of the homemade dough. Use 6 sheets of phyllo, brushing each sheet with oil, and laying one over the other. Place the phyllo in a deep pan and allow the ends to hang over the edges. Scoop in the filling and fold the edges towards the center. Brush with oil and bake in a 350 degrees F. for 25 minutes.

Preparation

Dough:

Pour the flour in a bowl. Add salt and 3 table-spoons of the oil. Rub mixture by hand until the flour and oil are well combined. Dissolve the yeast in ¼ cup of the warm water and add sugar to activate the yeast. When the yeast starts to rise, add it to the flour mixture and mix by hand. Add remaining ¼ cup of warm water and knead the dough. If it is too sticky, add 2 more tablespoons of flour; if it is too stiff, add 1 more tablespoon of water. Pour remaining 1 tablespoon oil in the bowl while kneading the dough. Keep folding the dough and kneading until it feels smooth. Cover dough with a dish towel and leave it to rise for 1 hour.

(Continued on page 137)

Filling and dough for Rice in a Curtain

RICE IN A CURTAIN (CONTINUED)

Rice:

2 cups white basmati rice

¼ cup vegetable oil plus more for brushing the dough

1 teaspoon salt

½ teaspoon saffron threads

½ cup frozen peas

½ cup chopped carrots

1 teaspoon Arabian Spice (page 22)

Meat Dressing for rice (page 133)

Almond and Raisin Dressing (page 132)

Rice:

In a pot, sauté rice in oil for about 3 minutes to coat with oil; add salt and stir. Add 3½ cups of water and bring to a boil. Add saffron threads. When water is almost absorbed, stir in the peas, carrots and spice blend. Lower the heat and simmer until the rice grains are tender. Remove from heat and stir in the two dressings. Set aside.

Assemble the dish:

Preheat the oven to 375 degrees F. Brush a medium pot or a deep spring-form pan with oil and set aside. Using a rolling pin on a floured board, roll out the dough large enough to line the pan with enough overhang to cover the top of the rice filling. Lift the dough and line the oiled pan with it letting dough hang over the sides. Scoop in the rice mixture to fill the dough. Fold in the edges of the dough towards the center and seal dough closed over the rice mixture. Brush with oil.

Bake rice dish for 35 minutes. Remove the pan from the oven and leave it to cool for 30 minutes. Place a large tray or a platter on top of the pan and flip the pan over onto the platter and release (just like flipping a cake onto a dish). Serve with vegetable stew and a salad.

BULGUR WITH CHICKPEAS
BURGHER BIL HUMMUS

4 servings

We traditionally add bulgur to partially cooked chicken or lamb and let them finish cooking together. But with that method the outcome of this pilaf is sticky. I found a better way to cook bulgur. I drop it in boiling water for a few minutes and then drain it to discard the starches. Then I add it to the sauce or vegetables I have prepared to finish cooking together. The outcome is nice and fluffy!

Ingredients

3 tablespoons olive oil

1 small onion, chopped

1 teaspoon salt

1 teaspoon Arabian Spice (page 22)

½ cup tomato sauce

1 cup canned chickpeas, rinsed and
   drained

1½ cups coarse bulgur (no. 3 or 4)

Variation: You can use frozen peas instead of chickpeas.

Preparation

Heat olive oil in a pot and sauté onion; add salt, spice blend, and tomato sauce. Add the chickpeas and ½ cup of water and simmer for 5 minutes.

Fill another saucepan with water and bring to a boil. Add the bulgur and simmer for 10 minutes. Remove from heat and pour in the colander to drain.

Add the cooked bulgur to the onion mixture. Add another ½ cup of water and simmer on low heat for 15 minutes. Remove from heat and fluff. Serve with Yogurt Cucumber Salad (page 114) or pickles.

BULGUR WITH MUSHROOMS

BURGHER BIL FTIR

4 servings

Mushrooms are a relatively new ingredient on the Iraqi culinary landscape. We have incorporated them into Iraqi recipes to replace truffles (chema) that are only available in the market for two weeks a year. Mushrooms have a similar texture as truffles when cooked and they are available in the market year round.

Ingredients

3 tablespoons olive oil

1 medium onion, chopped

½ teaspoon salt

1 teaspoon Arabian Spice (page 22)

1 pound button mushrooms, sliced

½ cup tomato sauce

1½ cups coarse bulgur (no. 3 or 4), rinsed

Preparation

Heat oil in a pot and sauté the onion. Add salt and spice blend.

Add the mushrooms to the onions and cook for 10 minutes. Add tomato sauce and 1 cup of water and stir. Simmer for 5 minutes.

Meanwhile, fill a pot with water, add some salt, and bring to a boil. Add bulgur and simmer for 10 minutes, uncovered. Drain in a colander.

Add bulgur to the mushroom mixture and stir. Simmer on low heat until all the sauce is absorbed by the bulgur. Fluff with a big spoon.

Serve with Yogurt Cucumber Salad (page 114) or Yogurt Dill Sauce (page 115).

BULGUR WITH CHICKEN

BURGHER BIL DIJAJ

This recipe is very popular in northern Iraq. In Mosul, they sometimes use wild quail birds called qata *instead of chicken.*

Ingredients

1 whole chicken

1 teaspoon salt

1 teaspoon Arabian Spice (page 22)

1 cup tomato sauce

2 cups coarse bulgur (no.4), rinsed and drained

1 (15-ounce) can chickpeas, rinsed and drained

1 medium onion, chopped

2 tablespoons olive oil

Preparation

Place the chicken in a deep pot. Sear the chicken over low heat on all sides for 10 minutes. Add salt, spice blend, tomato sauce, and 4 cups of water. Bring to a boil, then reduce the heat and simmer for 40 minutes, until the chicken is cooked. Remove the chicken from the sauce. Take meat off bones and discard the bones. Set aside.

Add the bulgur and chickpeas to the sauce. Bring to a boil and reduce the heat. Simmer, covered, until the sauce is completely absorbed.

Sauté the onion in the olive oil and add to the bulgur and fluff.

Serve the bulgur on a plate topped with pieces of chicken. Serve with Arabic Salad (page 105) or Yogurt Cucumber Salad (page 114).

CREAM OF WHEAT, BULGUR, AND LAMB DISKS

OQ TSHISHI / IROOG JIREESH

Makes 6 disks

For this recipe, you'll need to prepare the two layers separately and then assemble the disks. You can substitute semolina for cream of wheat if desired. This is another recipe that originated in Mosul, since bulgur is plentiful in the north and people are very creative in using it in a variety of recipes.

Ingredients

Wheat Layer:

2 cups cream of wheat (*jireesh*) or
    semolina

1 cup fine grade bulgur

¾ pound ground lamb or beef with
    some fat

1 large onion, chopped

1 teaspoon salt

1 teaspoon Arabian Spice (page 22)

½ teaspoon curry powder

½ 6-ounce can tomato paste

2 tomatoes, chopped

Meat Layer:

1 pound ground lamb

1 onion, chopped

1 teaspoon salt

1 teaspoon Arabian Spice (page 22)

1 cup chopped tomatoes

½ 6-ounce can tomato paste

1 egg

1 tablespoon tomato paste

1 cup flour for the board

Variation: Instead of making individual disks, you can press all the wheat mixture in an oiled baking pan (13 x 9-inch) and cover with all meat mixture. Brush the top with the egg wash. Cut in diamond shapes and bake in a preheated oven at 375 degrees F for 35 minutes.

Preparation

Prepare the wheat layer:
In a large bowl, mix the cream of wheat and bulgur. Add 1½ cups of water and leave the mixture for 30 minutes to absorb the water. Squeeze out the water and discard. To the bulgur mixture add the ground lamb or beef, onion, salt, spice blend, and curry powder. Add the tomato paste and tomatoes and mix well. Set aside.

Prepare meat layer:
In a large bowl, combine ground lamb with onion, salt, spice blend, chopped tomatoes, and tomato paste. Mix well and set aside.

Assembly:
Preheat oven to 375 degrees F.

In a small bowl, mix together the 1 egg and 1 tablespoon tomato paste to make an egg wash. Divide the wheat mixture into 6 portions and the meat mixture into 6 portions. Make a large ball of one of the wheat portions and flatten it on a board sprinkled with flour to make a 5-inch wide circle. Make a ball of one of the meat portions and press it over the wheat disk. Brush the top with some of the egg wash to hold the top layer of meat together and give it a shiny surface when baked. Place in an oiled pan. Repeat with remaining wheat and meat portions. Bake for 35 minutes.

BARLEY PILAF WITH LAMB SHANKS

KASHKA-HABBIYA

6 to 8 servings

For this recipe, we use pearl barley, which is processed and polished to remove the outer layer of bran. It takes less time to cook.

Ingredients

2 tablespoons vegetable oil

3 pounds lamb shanks

1 (8-ounce) can tomato sauce or fresh tomato juice

1 teaspoon salt

1 teaspoon Arabian Spice (page 22)

1 (15-ounce) can chickpeas, rinsed and drained

2 cups pearl barley, rinsed and drained

2 tablespoons butter, divided

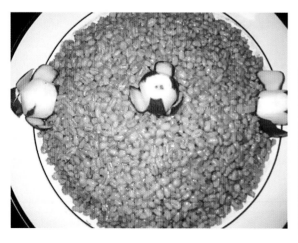

Preparation

In a pot, heat oil and brown the meat for 5 minutes. Add 6 cups of water, the tomato sauce, salt, and spice blend. Cover and simmer on low heat for 90 minutes.

When the shanks are tender, remove the meat from the sauce and set aside. Add the chickpeas and barley to the sauce. Make sure the sauce level is 2 inches above the level of the barley, and add some water if needed. Add 1 tablespoon of the butter. Bring to a boil and then reduce heat and simmer for 40 minutes, until the barley is tender and all the sauce is absorbed.

Sauté the cooked meat in the remaining 1 tablespoon of butter. Plate the barley pilaf on a serving dish and top it with the sautéed lamb. Serve with salad, radishes, and pickles.

Variations: You can add the barley to the meat when meat is partially cooked and they can cook together until done.

You can use turmeric to give the barley pilaf a yellow color in place of the tomato sauce which gives it a red color.

You can cook this recipe with chicken also.

STORING FOODS

Father went to the market every morning to buy meat, vegetables, and fruit carrying a shopping basket made of date palm tree leaves (*zanbeel*). In the early 1940s we did not have a refrigerator, so we used an icebox to keep the food and water cool. We had ice delivered every day and we washed the ice and wrapped it in a burlap cloth and placed it in the icebox. We did not keep leftover food. When the weather was cold, food was placed outside in a cupboard with a mesh wire.

We always stored grains, sugar, and flour in big sacks and placed them in a special room next to the kitchen called a *makhzan*. We bought onions and garlic by the bushel and kept them for the whole season. We bought okra during the summer, threaded it, and hung it to dry to use during winter. Clarified butter for cooking was kept in a big aluminum can or a pottery jar. Pottery urns were used for storing olives, pickles, date syrup (*dibis*), and sesame paste (*tahini*) that came from Mosul to Baghdad.

Every season, there were Kurdish street vendors pushing carts and making calls in the street. Mother used to go out to see what they brought from Mosul or the mountain areas in the North like Arbil and Sulaymaniya. Mostly, they brought nuts, grains, dried fruits like raisins and figs, *halawa*, tahini, a Kurdish cheese called *beiza* that was aged in sheepskin, and garlic cheese preserved in salt water.

When we purchased a refrigerator in 1952 life changed, and so did our shopping habits. We started doing our shopping once a week, but continued to shop for bread every day. People became more creative and my mother began using the freezer more. She froze the vegetables for consumption in winter and kept orange and lemon juice in the freezer. By the early 1970s, almost every home had acquired a freezer. We would fill the freezer with baked goods and all kinds of *kibbi* and pastries, meats, and vegetables so that when we had an unexpected guest (which happened very often) we were able to set a table in 40 minutes with all kinds of appetizing food. While my sisters and I were preparing the food in the kitchen (which was very roomy), my parents were entertaining the guests and catching up with their news. Guests were served an orange drink (*sharbat*) or a cup of Arabic coffee. Tea and dessert were served at the end of the meal.

KIBBI OR KUBBA

Kibbi is a special dumpling made with either bulgur or rice dough, stuffed with meat and chopped onions, and then boiled or baked in a sauce or fried. *Kibbi* can be shaped into patties, balls, or large discs. They are typically served as an appetizer but can be a main meal.

When I was a child, we used the meat grinder and the mortar and pestle to prepare the *kibbi* dough for stuffing. You can use the food processor for this purpose.

Rice *kibbi* is made with regular rice that has been soaked for an hour in water. You then drain the rice and pulse it in the food processor until it achieves the size and texture of cornmeal. We used to run it through the meat grinder a few times. Nowadays, I usually buy cream of rice in a box to use for rice *kibbi*. You can find it in the hot cereal section in the grocery stores.

My sister uses 2 cups of ground rice and 1 cup of extra lean ground beef to make her *kibbi*. Place them in the food processor with 1 teaspoon of salt and ⅓ cup of water. Pulse a few times until it becomes a pliable dough, but not too soft. Then you are ready to make the *kibbi*.

I have given some recipes for cooked rice *kibbi* (*Kibbat Halab*) in the appetizer section. On the following page is the recipe that I make with cream of rice and it is always very successful. It is followed by a few recipes for cooking the rice *kibbi* in a variety of soups. And they are followed by some recipes for *Kibbi Mosul*, a delicious variation using bulgur instead of rice.

Rice Kibbi in Tomato Sauce

RICE KIBBI

KIBBI TIMMAN

Makes 25 to 30 *kibbis*

Ingredients

Dough:

1 (14-ounce) box cream of rice cereal

¾ pound ground chuck

1 teaspoon salt

Filling:

1 pound ground lamb or ground
   chuck steak

½ teaspoon salt

½ teaspoon Arabian Spice (page 22)

½ onion, chopped

Preparation

Dough:
In a bowl, combine ½ cup of water with all the dough ingredients. Place half of the mixture in the food processor. Process, adding a little more water if needed, until it becomes a soft dough. Process the other half of the dough in the same manner and set aside.

Filling:
Combine all the filling ingredients in a bowl.

Assembly:
Take a small piece of dough the size of an egg. Shape it into a cup and fill it with 1 tablespoon of filling. Pinch the edges of the cup together to enclose the filling. Flatten it to make a small disk and put on a baking tray. Repeat until all dough and filling are used.

Cover with plastic wrap and freeze. or use in any of the recipes on the following pages.

RICE KIBBI IN LAMB SOUP

KIBBI YAKHNI

5 to 6 servings

We always prepare a big pot of this soup for Easter or Christmas. Our uncles and aunts would visit us after church service to wish us a happy holiday and of course they stayed for lunch. My mother would prepare the lamb soup and the rice kibbi *the day before, and when we came back from the church service she dropped the rice* kibbi *in the boiling soup.*

Ingredients

2 pounds lamb with bones

2 medium onions, sliced

1 tablespoon salt

1 (15.5-ounce) can chickpeas, drained

20 rice *kibbis* (page 147)

Preparation

Put lamb with bones, onions, salt, and 10 cups of water in a large pot. Bring to a boil and cook until the meat is tender.

Remove the bones and add chickpeas. (Soup can be made ahead of time to this point.)

When ready to cook the *kibbi*, bring the soup to a boil and then drop the rice *kibbis* in the soup and continue to boil partially covered. Add more salt to the soup if needed. When the *kibbis* rise to the top, they are done (about 20 minutes).

Serve this in soup bowls with bread and pickles on the side.

Note: Be sure to prepare the rice *kibbis* in advance.

RICE KIBBI IN SWISS CHARD SOUP

KIBBI HAMUTH BIL SILIG

5 to 6 servings

Swiss chard is a winter vegetable. Be sure to wash thoroughly to remove the sand and drain. You can substitute fresh spinach for the Swiss chard if you prefer.

Ingredients

1 pound lamb soup bones

1 large onion, sliced

½ cup rice

1 teaspoon salt

2 pounds Swiss chard, washed and chopped

5 cloves garlic, chopped

2 tablespoons tomato paste (optional)

20 to 25 rice *kibbis* (page 147)

1 tablespoon dried mint

1 tablespoon dried parsley

⅓ cup lemon juice

Note: Be sure to prepare the rice *kibbis* in advance.

Preparation

Place the lamb bones in a large pot with 8 cups of water and the onion, rice, and salt. Bring to a boil and cook for 40 minutes, removing the scum that forms on top of the boiling water.

Remove the bones. Add the Swiss chard, garlic, and tomato paste to the pot. Bring to a boil. Reduce the heat and simmer for 10 minutes.

At this point, you can add the rice *kibbi* to the soup. Add more water if needed. Cover and cook for 20 minutes. When the *kibbis* float to the top of the soup, they are cooked.

Add the mint, parsley, and lemon juice. Adjust the salt and lemon as needed. Turn off the heat and leave the pot cover half open to release the steam.

RICE KIBBI IN TOMATO SAUCE

KIBBI HAMUTH

We usually add seasonal vegetables to this kibbi *sauce. In the summer we add zucchini, and in the winter we add turnips (shalgham).*

Ingredients

1 pound lamb soup bones

1 large onion, sliced

3 zucchini, peeled and sliced

1 (16-ounce) can tomato sauce

1 tablespoon tomato paste

4 cloves garlic, crushed

Juice of 3 lemons

1 tablespoon salt

20 small rice *kibbis* (page 147)

1 tablespoon dried mint

1 tablespoon dried parsley

Note: Be sure to prepare the rice *kibbis* in advance.

Preparation

Put 8 cups of water, lamb bones, and onions in a large pot and bring to a boil. Reduce heat, cover, and cook for 50 minutes.

Add the zucchini, tomato sauce, tomato paste, garlic, lemon juice, and salt. Simmer for 15 more minutes. Remove the lamb bones.

Drop the rice *kibbis* in the soup and bring to a boil. When they float to the top, add the mint and parsley. Cook for 10 more minutes partially covered. Serve in soup bowls with *tannour* bread or *saj* bread on the side.

SWEET RICE KIBBI SOUP

KIBBI ZIBIBIYI

6 to 8 servings

This sweet kibbi soup was usually served for the New Year lunch after the church service, when our uncles, aunts, and cousins visited to wish us a Happy New Year. Other dishes such as leg of lamb on top of a bed of saffron rice with raisins and toasted almonds, a vegetable stew, a big platter of dolma, salads, heavy appetizers, and pickles were also served . Use only rice kibbis for this recipe, and do not put onions in the stuffing. You can also stuff a few kibbis with walnuts instead. Whoever gets the walnut kibbi will have a good New Year!

Ingredients

3 pounds lamb shanks

1 cup dried dates (*qasib*)

½ cup golden raisins

1 teaspoon salt

½ teaspoon ground allspice

3 cinnamon sticks

5 whole cardamom pods

½ cup walnut halves

½ cup whole blanched almonds

½ cup date syrup (*dibis*, page 67)

⅓ cup lemon juice

20 rice *kibbis* made without onions
    (page 147)

3 tablespoons dried parsley

> **Note:** Be sure to prepare
> the rice *kibbis* in advance.

Preparation

In a large pot, cook the lamb shanks in 10 cups of water for 50 minutes. When meat is tender and falling off bones, remove the bones. Add the dates, raisins, salt, allspice, cinnamon sticks, cardamom pods, and nuts. Add date syrup and lemon juice. Bring to a boil and cook for 20 minutes. Remove the cinnamon sticks.

Drop the rice *kibbis* in the soup and cook, half covered, for 20 minutes. Add parsley and serve in soup bowls with bread on the side

BULGUR KIBBI

KIBBI MOSUL

Kibbi Mosul *is bulgur dough mixed with meat and filled with meat filling. It is flattened to make a circle about 6 to 9 inches in diameter. This* kibbi *originated in Mosul and became very popular in Baghdad during the 1960s when many families moved to Baghdad to escape the ethnic cleansing in Mosul. These families opened catering businesses, made different varieties of kibbi, and distributed them to restaurants and shops to stock their freezers.*

You can boil this kibbi *and freeze it, or freeze it uncooked. When we had unexpected guests, we took a kibbi Mosul out of the freezer and dropped it in salted boiling water and cooked for 10 minutes. We removed it from water and placed it on a plate and cut it into wedges. We usually serve it with a variety of pickles, sliced tomatoes, onions, radishes, and cucumbers.*

Every family has its own recipe for Kibbi Mosul. My mother uses the following recipe.

Ingredients

Bulgur dough:

4 cups fine grade bulgur, rinsed and drained

2 cups cream of wheat (*jireesh*) or semolina

1 pound lean ground beef

1 tablespoon salt

Filling:

1 medium onion

1 teaspoon salt

1 teaspoon Arabian Spice (page 22)

2 pounds ground lamb

Preparation

Dough:

Combine all the ingredients with ¾ cup of water in a big bowl. Place in a food processor and process to a soft dough, adding a little more water if needed. (You can run it through a meat grinder, but I prefer to use the food processor.) Set aside.

Filling:

Chop the onion, sprinkle it with the salt and spice blend, and let it stand for 30 minutes to wilt. Add the lamb and mix well.

Assembly:

Cover the work surface with plastic wrap and brush with water. Make 2 small balls the size of oranges from the dough. Place 1 of the balls on the plastic wrap and cover with another

(Recipe continued on following pages)

BULGUR KIBBI (CONTINUED)

layer of wrap. Roll the dough flat with a rolling pin a little larger than 6 inches. Uncover and put a 6-inch round plate on top of the disk and cut a circle. Cover the circle with a handful of the filling, and spread it evenly keeping the filling a ½ inch from the edges of the circle. Roll out and cut the other ball of dough in the same manner and place it on top of the filling. Press the edges to seal the filling well. Repeat the process until the dough and filling are used (it makes about 6 to 8 *kibbis*).

Put the *kibbis* on a tray and store in the freezer for future use; or cook immediately in a pot of boiling water with salt. When the disk rises to the top, in about 10 minutes, take it out with a slotted spoon and place it on a plate. Cut into wedges like pizza.

Variation: You can make small *kibbi* bulgur to use for other recipes. Shape them in small disks as you do for the rice *kibbi* (page 147). These are used in the recipe for Bulgar Kibbi with Eggplant (page 157). The smaller versions can also be fried in a skillet for another delicious variation (see photo page 156).

Bulgur Kibbi
with Eggplant

Fried bulgur kibbi

BULGUR KIBBI WITH EGGPLANT

KIBBI BADINJAN

You can buy tamarind sauce in a jar in most stores. If you are using concentrated tamarind sauce, you need to put 1 tablespoon in ½ cup of boiling water and stir before adding to the kibbi sauce. For variation, you can use pomegranate syrup sold in a bottle. Use 2 to 3 tablespoons to flavor the sauce in place of the tamarind sauce.

Ingredients

2 large eggplants (about 3 pounds)

1 teaspoon salt

2 cups vegetable oil, divided

20 prepared small bulgur *kibbi* (see note below)

2 onions, sliced

2 tomatoes, sliced

1 (8-ounce) can tomato sauce

½ cup tamarind sauce

½ teaspoon curry powder

1 teaspoon Arabian Spice (page 22)

Note: For this recipe, use the Bulgur *Kibbi* (*Kibbi Mosul*) recipe (page 153) to make small bulgur *kibbi* disks in advance, following the instructions for the rice *kibbi* (page 147) to shape them.

Preparation

Preheat oven to 375 degrees F.

Slice eggplants crosswise into about ½-inch thick slices, salt them and place in a colander in the sink for 30 minutes to drain. Remove eggplant and place on a paper towel. Fry the eggplant slices in ¾ cup of oil on both sides and set aside.

In a deep pan, heat 1 cup of oil and fry the small *kibbi* until they are crispy on both sides and set aside. Discard oil.

Sauté onions in remaining ¼ cup of oil. Make a stack of an eggplant slice, *kibbi*, tomato slice, and onion slice and put in a deep 9x13-inch baking pan. Continue the process until all vegetables and *kibbis* are stacked and in the pan.

In a bowl mix ¾ cup of water with the tomato sauce and tamarind sauce and pour over the ingredients in pan. Sprinkle with some salt and the curry powder and spice blend. Cover the pan with foil and bake for at least 35 minutes, checking to see if it needs more water.

VEGETARIAN
DISHES

Vegetarian Dishes

Vegetables are a major part of the Iraqi cuisine. We cook them every day as stews and serve them with bread and over rice. I find these recipes very appealing because they are quick and easy to cook and economical.

Farmers markets (*alwa*), where we shop weekly for most of our food at reasonable prices, are scattered throughout the districts of Baghdad and other cities. Bargaining is a custom, and picking through the colorful baskets of fruits and vegetables to choose the perfect produce is acceptable and even expected. Vendors use a manual scale (*mizan*) where they put the vegetables on one side and the weights on the other side.

While neighborhood shops provide fruits and vegetables and we use them when we need something quickly, the downside is that they do not allow customers to pick through the baskets for the choicest fruit. Fruit and vegetable vendors also walk through the neighborhoods with their pushcarts daily, calling out the names of the vegetables they are selling, and we make sure to check their produce and purchase extra to make pickles or prepare them for the freezer for later use.

Many Iraqis started to cook vegetarian dishes as entrées due to the economical hardships and political sanctions that prevented shipments of food from being transported to major cities. They are also prepared during Lent. I wanted to present these recipes here for those who are on a vegetarian diet or on a moderate budget. You can use fresh seasonal or frozen vegetables for most of these dishes.

BOILED FAVA BEANS

BAGILLA KHATHRA

This summer vegetable (legume) can be found in most Iraqi home gardens and is used fresh or dry in many recipes. They look a lot like green beans but wider and are also called broad beans. You can find the fresh fava bean pods and frozen fava beans in Middle Eastern and Asian stores. Each pod contains between 4 to 6 beans. We cook the whole pods and snack on the flesh and beans using our hands. For this recipe I use fava bean pods. In other recipes, I shell the bean pods and remove the outer skin of the bean.

Ingredients

1 pound fresh fava beans

1 teaspoon salt

Preparation

Wash the beans and place them in a deep pan. Pour 2 cups of water over them. Place a heat-proof dessert plate over the beans to keep them submerged. Bring to a boil. Reduce the heat and simmer for 20 minutes. When beans are almost tender, sprinkle with salt and cook for 10 more minutes. Serve these beans with kababs or as a side dish to other meat dishes.

Note: These beans are a favorite snack sold by street vendors when fresh fava beans are in season.

FAVA BEAN STEW

BAJILLA BIL TAMATA

In this recipe you use the whole fava bean pods with the outer skin. Make sure to choose small and tender pods.

Ingredients

1 pound fresh fava bean pods

1 medium onion, chopped

2 tablespoons vegetable oil

1 large tomato, chopped

1 tablespoon tomato paste

1 teaspoon salt

1 teaspoon Arabian Spice (page 22)

Juice of 1 lemon

Preparation

Cut the ends off each fava bean pod and remove the strings. Slice the bean pods into ½-inch slices.

In a deep pan, sauté onion in oil and add the chopped tomato and tomato paste. Cook for 5 minutes. Add the fava bean slices, salt, and spice blend. Pour in 1½ cups water and bring to a boil. Reduce the heat to medium and simmer for 20 minutes, until the fava beans are tender.

Add lemon juice and more salt if needed. Serve beans with plain white rice and bread.

GREEN BEANS WITH TOMATOES

FASULIA KHATHRA

4 servings

If you are using fresh green beans, wash them and drain in a strainer. Cut off the two ends of each bean and cut each bean in two or three pieces. Cut mature beans in the French style if desired.

Ingredients

1 large onion, sliced

⅓ cup extra-virgin olive oil

1 teaspoon salt

1 teaspoon Arabian Spice (page 22)

1 pound fresh or frozen green beans

2 tomatoes, diced

1 (8-ounce) can tomato sauce

Preparation

In a deep pan, sauté the onions in olive oil for 5 minutes. Sprinkle with salt and spice blend. Add the beans, diced tomatoes, tomato sauce, and 1 ½ cups water. Cover and bring to a boil. Lower heat to medium and simmer for about 20 minutes, until beans are tender. Serve with rice.

WHITE BEANS IN TOMATO SAUCE

FASULIA BEITHA

6 to 8 servings

We usually prepare this dish during winter when fresh vegetables are scarce. It makes a meal by itself when served with bread as a thick soup or over a bowl of white rice.

Ingredients

2 cups dried white beans

4 tablespoons olive oil

1 cup chopped onions

6 cups boiling water

1 teaspoon salt

1 teaspoon Arabian Spice (page 22)

2 (8-ounce) cans tomato sauce

Chopped onion to decorate

1 tablespoon vinegar (optional)

Preparation

Soak the beans in a bowl of water to cover for 6 hours or overnight. Drain the beans and discard the water.

Heat the oil in a large pot and sauté the onions for 5 minutes. Add the beans and boiling water and bring back to a boil. Lower the heat and cook for 40 minutes.

When the beans are soft, add the salt, spice blend, and tomato sauce and bring back to a boil. Lower heat and simmer, covered, for 25 minutes. Make sure to stir it every now and then to prevent the beans from sticking to the bottom of the pot.

Serve with plain white rice. Top with chopped onions and 1 tablespoon of vinegar.

RICE WITH CARROTS

TIMMAN BIL JIZAR

4 to 6 servings

Carrots are root vegetables and are abundant during winter in Iraq. They come in a variety of colors: yellow, purple, and orange. We snack on them, boil them, pickle them, and cook them in a variety of dishes. I use orange carrots for this recipe. Make sure to buy the carrots with green tops attached to them to ensure freshness and a sweet taste.

Ingredients

1 cup chopped carrots

1 medium onion, chopped

3 tablespoons vegetable oil

1 teaspoon salt

1 teaspoon Arabian Spice (page 22)

1 cup rice, rinsed and drained

½ cup frozen peas

Pickles and sliced tomatoes for
   decoration

Variations: You can add 1 cup of chopped mushrooms with the onions and sauté them together.

Sometimes we add chopped truffles (*chema*) when they are in season.

Preparation

In a pot, bring 2 cups of water to a boil. Add the carrots and cook for 10 minutes. Remove the carrots with a slotted spoon and reserve the water to use when cooking the rice.

In the meantime, in another pot, sauté the onion in oil until soft and then add the salt and spice blend. Add carrots to the onion mixture, and sauté for 5 minutes.

Add the rice to the onion and carrot mixture. Sauté the rice with the vegetables for 3 minutes. Add reserved carrot water and bring to a boil half covered. When the water is almost absorbed, about 20 minutes, lower the heat. Stir the frozen peas into the rice mixture. Cover and simmer until the rice is tender.

Fluff the rice with a big spoon and leave the pot lid halfway open to let the steam out for 10 minutes. Serve with pickles and sliced tomatoes.

FRIED EGGPLANT

BADINJAN MIQLI

4 servings

This is a very basic eggplant recipe that we make as a side dish to serve with chicken, kababs, red rice, or in a sandwich. In the U.S., I find a variety of eggplant sizes and shapes. The most common eggplant we use in Iraq is the Italian eggplant. It is about 5 inches long and we usually fry it or stuff it. For this recipe I use a large eggplant like the ones that you find in regular U.S. grocery stores.

Ingredients

1 large eggplant (about 1½ pounds)

1 teaspoon salt

¼ cup vegetable oil plus more if needed

3 tablespoons apple cider vinegar

1 clove garlic, sliced

¼ cup chopped parsley for decoration

Preparation

Remove the stem from the eggplant. Peel the eggplant lengthwise in half inch strips. Cut the eggplant crosswise or lengthwise into thin slices and place in a colander in a sink. Sprinkle with salt and leave to drain for 45 minutes. Remove the eggplant slices from the colander and dry with paper towel.

Heat the oil in a sauté pan on medium heat. Slide the eggplant slices into the oil and fry them until lightly browned on both sides. Remove from the pan and drain on paper towels.

Arrange the eggplant slices on a plate. Drizzle the vinegar over them. Decorate them with sliced garlic and chopped parsley.

Variation: For a lighter version, you can eliminate the frying process. Drizzle olive oil over the eggplants and place them on a baking sheet under the broiler for 7 minutes or until they are lightly browned. Turn the slices and repeat on other side. Serve as described.

STUFFED CABBAGE LEAVES

MAHSHI LAHANA

6 to 8 servings

Green cabbage grows during winter in Iraq. We do not have the purple and Chinese cabbage varieties. I have tried using Chinese cabbage leaves for this recipe and they work fine. Chinese cabbage is silky, tender, and does not take a long time to cook. Make sure not to roll the cabbage up too tightly to allow room for the rice grains to expand while cooking. Otherwise the leaves will burst or the rice grains will not fully cook.

Ingredients

1½ cups white rice

4 tablespoons olive oil

1 large onion, chopped

3 cloves garlic, chopped

1 teaspoon salt

½ teaspoon Arabian Spice (page 22)

1 tablespoon dried mint

½ cup chopped fresh dill

1 head white cabbage

1 cup tomato sauce

Juice of 1 lemon

Yogurt Dill Sauce (page 115)

Preparation

Prepare filling:
Rinse the rice and place it in a colander. In a deep pan, heat the oil and sauté the onion and garlic for a few minutes. Add the salt, spice blend, and rice and sauté for 5 minutes. Add the mint and dill. Remove from the pan to cool.

Prepare cabbage:
Bring a large pot of water to a boil. Add the cabbage head with the core down. Cover the pot and simmer on low heat for 20 minutes. Remove the head of cabbage from the pot and place in a colander to cool. When cool, separate the leaves and place them on a cutting board.

Assembly:
Cut the middle thick vein from each cabbage leaf and separate the two parts of the leaf. Place 1 tablespoon of the filling on a leaf half. Fold the leaf over the filling and fold the edges towards the center and roll the leaf loosely. Repeat with remaining cabbage and filling. Arrange the cabbage rolls in a deep pan with

seam sides down. Mix together the tomato sauce, lemon juice, and 3 cups water and pour over the rolls. Place a heatproof dessert plate on top of the rolls to keep them submerged.

Bring to a boil over medium heat and cook for 15 minutes. Lower the heat, cover, and simmer for 30 more minutes or until the rice is cooked. Serve with Yogurt Dill Sauce.

STUFFED GRAPE LEAVES AND VEGETABLES

DOLMA BIL ZAIT

8 to 10 servings

You can purchase grape leaves in a jar from Middle Eastern grocery stores, or you can cut fresh leaves from the grapevine. Pick 30 to 40 medium-size grape leaves. You need to wash them and put them in a bowl of hot water for five minutes to wilt. Cool before rolling them. Sometimes we use Swiss chard instead of grape leaves for this recipe, especially during winter. Make sure not to over stuff the vegetables with the filling in order to allow room for the rice grains to expand while cooking. Otherwise the vegetables will burst or the rice grains will not fully cook.

Ingredients

Vegetables:

2 small zucchini

2 small Italian eggplants

2 small green peppers

2 medium onions

1 (16-ounce) jar grape leaves

⅓ cup lemon juice

Filling:

¼ cup olive oil

1 cup chopped onions

4 cloves garlic, chopped

2 teaspoons salt, divided

1 teaspoon Arabian Spice (page 22)

½ cup frozen peas

3 tablespoons pine nuts

3 tablespoons golden raisins

1 (8-ounce) can tomato sauce

1 cup white rice

Preparation

Peel the zucchinis and cut off the ends of the zucchini and eggplants and cut each in half crosswise. Core them to remove some of the flesh leaving a shell for stuffing and salt the inside. Chop the flesh and set aside to add to the filling.

Cut off the tops of the green peppers and reserve, and remove the seeds.

Cut the top off the onions and make a cut to the center. Put in hot water for 15 minutes. When soft, separate the onion layers for stuffing.

Make the filling: In a skillet, heat the oil and sauté the onions and garlic. Add 1 teaspoon salt and spice blend. Add the chopped flesh of the zucchini and eggplants and cook for 5 minutes. Stir in the peas, pine nuts, and raisins. Add the tomato sauce and rice. Stir the mixture for 5 minutes and then set aside to cool.

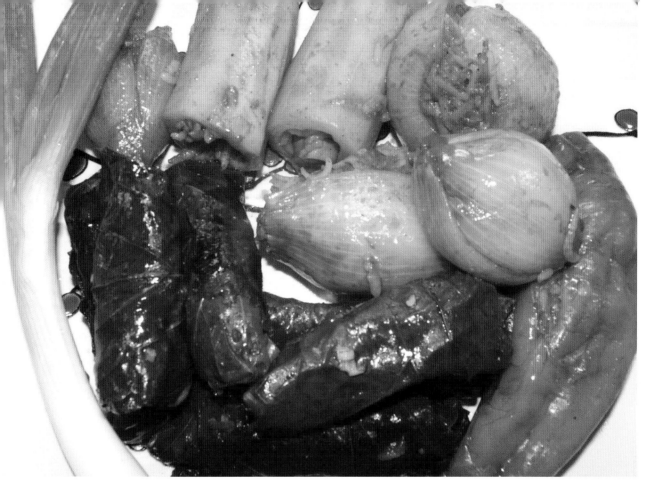

Stuff the cavities of the eggplants, zucchini, and onions with the filling and arrange in a deep pan. Stuff the 2 green pepper cups, replace the tops and put in the pan also.

Remove the grape leaves from the jar and rinse them. Arrange them on a cutting board. Put 1 tablespoon of the filling on the stem side of a leaf. Roll the leaf over the filling. Turn the sides of the leaf towards the center, and roll the leaf to the end. Repeat with remaining leaves and filling. Arrange the stuffed grape leaves on top of the vegetables. Place a heatproof plate on top to keep them submerged in the water.

Mix 1½ cups water and the lemon juice and pour over the stuffed vegetables. Bring to a boil. Reduce the heat and simmer for 35 minutes, until the rice is cooked and the vegetables are tender.

To serve this dish, place a big plate or tray on top of the pot and flip the pot over onto the tray and remove. Serve with Yogurt Cucumber Salad (page 114) and *tannour* bread.

CAULIFLOWER WITH TOMATOES

QARNABEET BIL TAMATA

4 to 6 servings

Cauliflower is a winter vegetable. The white variety grows in Iraq, but you could also use the green or purple variety that you find in the farmers market in the U.S. Sometimes brown spots develop on the florets when stored for a few weeks in the refrigerator. Make sure to cut the brown discoloration off before you cook the cauliflower.

Ingredients

2 tablespoons olive oil

½ cup chopped onions

3 cups chopped cauliflower

2 tomatoes, diced

1 teaspoon salt

½ teaspoon Arabian Spice (page 22)

1 tablespoon tomato paste

Juice of ½ lemon

Preparation

Heat oil in a large skillet. Sauté onions in oil until softened and then add cauliflower. Cook for 5 minutes.

Add 1 cup of water, tomatoes, salt, and spice blend. Bring to a boil. Reduce heat and add the tomato paste. Simmer for 15 minutes.

Pour the lemon juice over the cauliflower and turn off the heat. Serve as a side dish with bulgur or plain white rice.

OKRA STEW

BAMIA BIL ZEIT

4 to 6 servings

Okra is a favorite summer vegetable in Iraq. We serve this dish with plain white rice. When we serve it in a soup bowl with tannour *bread, we call it* thireed bamya. *People even eat this delicious okra stew for breakfast!*

Ingredients

4 cloves garlic, sliced

2 tablespoons olive oil

1 cup tomato sauce

1 pound fresh or frozen whole okra

1 teaspoon salt

Juice of 1 lemon

Preparation

Sauté the garlic in oil until starting to soften and then add the tomato sauce and bring to a boil. Add the okra and 2 cups of water and bring to a boil. Reduce heat and simmer for 20 minutes. Season with salt and add lemon juice. Simmer for 10 more minutes.

Note: When you buy fresh okra, you need to trim off the stems and wash them before cooking. If you like to keep a supply in the freezer for winter, you can buy fresh okra, blanch it in boiling salted water for 5 minutes, drain, pour ice water over, then spread on a tray to cool and bag it in freezer bags. These days you can also find frozen whole okra in the freezer section in most grocery stores.

ZUCCHINI WITH TOMATOES

TAPSI / TAWAT SHIJAR

4 to 6 servings

You can use fresh yellow squash for this recipe, too.

Ingredients

¼ cup olive oil

1 large onion, sliced

4 cloves garlic, sliced

1 large tomato, sliced

1 teaspoon salt

1 teaspoon Arabian Spice (page 22)

4 to 5 medium zucchini, peeled and cut in ½-inch-thick slices

1 (8-ounce) can tomato sauce

Preparation

Heat the oil in a deep sauté pan. Add the onion and garlic and cook and stir for 5 minutes. Arrange the tomato slices on top of the onions. Sprinkle with salt and spice blend. Add the zucchini in one layer and spread the tomato sauce over top. Cover the pan and simmer for 5 minutes.

Pour 1 cup of water over the zucchini and bring to a boil. Reduce the heat and simmer for 20 minutes, until the zucchini are tender. Serve with plain white rice.

POTATOES WITH PEAS

BATATA BIL BAZALIA

This is one of my son's favorite meals that he wants me to prepare for him at least once a week. My mother used to fry the potatoes before adding them to the sauce. I prefer to eliminate the frying process and make it a lighter meal.

Ingredients

4 large potatoes

1 large onion, chopped

¼ cup vegetable oil

4 cloves garlic, chopped

1 teaspoon salt

2 tablespoons curry powder

1 (8-ounce) can diced tomatoes

2 tablespoons tomato paste

1 tablespoon ground dried lime

Juice of 1 lemon

1 cup frozen peas

Preparation

Peel the potatoes and slice them into ½-inch-thick slices. Set aside.

Sauté the onions in oil until they soften. Add the garlic, salt, and curry powder, and stir for 3 minutes. Pour the diced tomatoes over the onions and simmer for 5 minutes. Add the sliced potatoes and stir.

Dilute the tomato paste in 2 cups of water and add to the pot. Add the dried lime and lemon juice and bring to a boil. Lower the heat and simmer the potatoes for 20 minutes. Add the frozen peas and cook for 10 more minutes.

Serve over Rice with Noodles (page 122) or Saffron Rice (page 123).

Vegetables with Meat Patties

MEATS WITH VEGETABLES

Meats with Vegetables

The typical Iraqi meal consists of a meat stew cooked with vegetables and served with rice and bread on the side. A variety of dried beans are cooked with meat also. Lamb is very expensive but the most favored meat in Iraq. We use lamb shoulder, lamb chops, and stewing beef for vegetable stews. Iraqi beef can be used in recipes interchangeably with lamb. Leg of lamb is chopped into cubes for kabab, *tikka*, and *kibbi* dishes. Ground lamb is mixed with ground beef for all the ground meat (*qeema*) dishes.

When we make the weekly visit to the butcher to get the supply of meat, we choose the cuts of meat we need for that week. Each family shops at their favorite butcher, and the butcher keeps the best cuts for his loyal customers. Usually, a one-year-old lamb that weighs 30 to 40 pounds is preferred to the older and heavier lamb. When we bring the meat home, we sort out the cuts and store them in the freezer for the meals planned for the week.

LAMB SHANKS WITH WHITE BEAN STEW

FASULIA BEITHA BIL LAHAM

4 to 6 servings

For this recipe, you need to purchase whole dried limes or crushed dried limes. You can find them in Asian or Middle Eastern grocery stores. We call them noomi basra, *and they are also called* omani lime. *When using whole limes, make sure to crush them and remove the seeds since they give a bitter flavor to the sauce. When cooking beans, make sure to add salt last, after the beans are cooked. If you add salt to beans in the beginning, they tend to harden and take a long time to cook.*

Ingredients

1 pound white dried beans

4 lamb shanks

2 tablespoons vegetable oil

1 large onion, chopped

2 tablespoons tomato paste

1 (8-ounce) can tomato sauce

2 dried limes (*noomi basra*), rinsed, crushed, and seeded

1 teaspoon salt

½ teaspoon Arabian Spice (page 22)

Preparation

In a large bowl, soak the white beans overnight in water to cover. Drain the beans.

In a pot, sauté the lamb shanks in oil to brown. Add onion and 8 cups of water and bring to a boil. Simmer, covered, on low heat for 1 hour.

When shanks are tender, add the beans, and cook for 20 minutes. When beans are soft, add tomato paste, tomato sauce, dried limes, salt, and spice blend. Cook for 30 more minutes. Serve with plain white rice.

Qeema with split peas is always prepared and served over rice during the month of Muharram (forbidden to kill). Traditionally it is the men's job to cook this meal in large pots outdoors and to keep stirring it to make sure the chickpeas are mashed. It is served for the congregation after the prayer service at the mosque. People donate food and desserts to the mosques and neighbors send plates of food to their neighbors in memory of Imam Al Hussein.

Ashura means the 10th day of Muharram commemorating the martyrdom of Imam Al Husseln lbn All, the grandson of the prophet Mohammed, in the battle of Karbala in 680 CE. This holiday is observed by the Shia communities throughout the world. Every year Shias make the pilgrimage to the shrine in Karbala which is located south of Baghdad.

SPLIT CHICKPEA AND LAMB STEW

MARGAT QEEMA

6 servings

The term qeema refers to ground beef or lamb sautéed with chopped onions. If you use ground lamb or beef, the recipe takes a short time to cook. I prefer using stewing meat and then shredding the meat once it is cooked. This is a traditional recipe cooked specifically during the holy month of Muharram which is the first month of the Islamic Lunar Year.

Ingredients

1 cup dried split chickpeas, soaked
   overnight

2 pounds lamb, cut in cubes

3 tablespoons vegetable oil

1 large onion, chopped

1 teaspoon salt

1 teaspoon Arabian Spice (page 22)

2 tablespoons tomato paste

3 whole dried lime (*noomi Basra*),
   broken in half and seeds removed

Note: *You can find dried split chickpeas in Middle Eastern and Asian grocery stores, or use canned chickpeas to save time. If using canned chickpeas, make sure to drain and rinse them first and there is no need to soak them overnight or precook them.*

Preparation

Drain the soaked dried split chickpeas and put them in a pot of boiling water. Cook for 15 minutes. Drain and set aside. (Do not add salt to the boiling water otherwise it will take a long time for chickpeas to cook.)

In a deep pot, sauté the lamb in the vegetable oil and add onion, salt, and spice blend. Stir a few times until onions become translucent. Add tomato paste and 6 cups of water and bring to a boil. Reduce heat and simmer for 1 hour, until lamb is tender.

Shred the meat in the pot using two forks. Add the chickpeas and dried limes. Bring the stew to a boil. Reduce heat and simmer for 20 minutes. Make sure to stir the pot while cooking to prevent it from sticking to the bottom of the pot and burning.

Mash the split chickpeas in the stew using a potato masher to make a thick stew. Serve over plain white rice.

OKRA WITH LAMB

BAMYA BIL LAHAM

This is a very traditional recipe enjoyed by all Iraqis. We plant okra in the garden during the summer, and then we harvest it when it is about one inch long. We keep a few bags in the freezer to cook during winter. In the early days before we had a freezer, we dried okra to cook for winter. You can find okra in the frozen vegetables section of the grocery store when it is not in season in the U.S.

We serve this dish with white rice or pour it in a soup bowl with toasted bread in the bottom, when we call it tashreeb bamya. *I usually add lemon juice to this recipe, but my mother and sisters use summac juice to flavor it. I have tried tamarind or pomegranate syrup too, but they tend to give the okra stew a darker color.*

Ingredients

2 teaspoons vegetable oil

1 pound lamb chops

1 pound frozen whole okra

1 (16-ounce) can tomato sauce

6 cloves garlic, sliced

1 teaspoon salt

⅓ cup lemon juice

Preparation

In a pot, heat the oil and sauté the lamb until lightly browned on both sides. Add 4 cups of water to the pot and simmer, covered, for 40 minutes, until the lamb is tender.

Add okra, tomato sauce, garlic, and salt. Bring to a boil and then reduce the heat and simmer for 20 minutes, until the okra is cooked. Pour the lemon juice over the okra and simmer for 10 more minutes.

Taste to see if it needs more salt. This stew tastes better the following day. Serve it with rice and *tannour* bread.

PEAS WITH LAMB

BAZALIA

4 to 6 servings

During the summer, we purchase bushels of pea pods to prepare them for the freezer to use during winter. Young children help out in the kitchen by shelling the peas, while the adults blanch them and pack them in freezer bags for winter. A perfect way to save the summer's bounty!

Ingredients

2 tablespoons oil

1 pound lamb chops

1 medium onion, chopped

1 clove garlic, chopped

1 (16-ounce) can diced tomatoes

1 teaspoon salt

1 teaspoon Arabian Spice (page 22)

1 pound shelled fresh or frozen peas

Preparation

In a pot, heat the oil and brown lamb chops on both sides. Add onion, garlic, and 1½ cups of water and simmer for 30 minutes, covered, on medium heat.

Add diced tomatoes, salt, and spice blend. Cook for 10 more minutes or until lamb is tender. Add the peas and cook for 15 more minutes. Serve with white rice.

Variation: You can use ground beef or lamb instead of the lamb chops for this recipe. Sauté the meat and add onions, garlic, salt, and spices. Add the crushed tomatoes and peas and simmer for 20 minutes.

CABBAGE STEW

LAHANA BIL QEEMA

4 servings

Cabbage is a winter vegetable. We chop it and cook it with meat just like cauliflower. But we do not eat it uncooked in salads. Even when we pickle it, we blanch it in hot water before adding to the brine.

Ingredients

2 teaspoons oil

1 large onion, chopped

3 cloves garlic, crushed

1 pound ground beef or lamb

2 tablespoons tomato paste

1 teaspoon salt

1 teaspoon Arabian Spice (page 22)

½ head cabbage, chopped

1 tablespoon dried mint

Variation: You can substitute carrots or cauliflower for the cabbage.

Preparation

In a large skillet, heat oil and sauté the onion and garlic until soft . Add the meat and cook until browned. Add tomato paste, salt, and spice blend and stir. Add the chopped cabbage and dried mint and stir for 5 minutes. Pour in 1 cup of water and simmer, covered, until the cabbage leaves become soft, about 20 minutes. Serve with white rice.

STUFFED CABBAGE LEAVES

MAHSHI LAHANA

6 to 8 servings

We cook this dish in winter when cabbage is in season. Make sure to remove 2 or 3 outer leaves of the cabbage and the stem. In Iraq, we use green cabbage for this dish. Here in the U.S. I use Chinese or Napa cabbage since they are sweet, tender, and cook fast. Make sure not to roll the cabbage up too tightly to allow room for the rice grains to expand while cooking. Otherwise the leaves will burst or the rice grains will not fully cook.

Ingredients

1 pound ground chuck

1 medium onion, chopped

2 cloves garlic, chopped

1 teaspoon salt

1 teaspoon Arabian Spice (page 22)

1 teaspoon dried mint

1 cup rice, rinsed and drained

1 head cabbage

1 cup tomato sauce

Juice of 1 lemon

Preparation

In a large bowl, combine the ground chuck with the onion, garlic, salt, spice blend, and mint. Add the rice, mix well, and set aside.

Fill a big pot with enough water to cover the cabbage. Drop in the cabbage head with the core down. Cover the pot and bring to a boil. Lower heat and simmer for 15 minutes.

Remove the head of cabbage from the pot and place in a colander to cool. When cool, peel the leaves and place them on a cutting board. Remove the middle thick veins and separate the two parts of the leaves.

Place 1 tablespoon of the filling on a leaf half. Fold cabbage leaf over the filling, fold the edges toward the center, and roll the leaf loosely. Repeat with remaining filling and leaves. Arrange the cabbage rolls in a deep pan with the seam sides down.

Mix together the tomato sauce, lemon juice, and 3 cups of water and pour over the rolls. Place a heatproof dessert plate on top of the rolls to keep them submerged. Bring to a boil and cook for 15 minutes. Reduce the heat and simmer for 20 more minutes until the rice is cooked. Serve with Yogurt Cucumber Salad (page 114).

STUFFED ZUCCHINI

SHEIKH MAHSHI

6 servings

We call this dish Sheikh Mahshi *which means "stuffed sheikh." It is a very popular dish during the summer when the vegetables are plentiful.*

Ingredients

4 medium zucchini

1 tablespoon vegetable oil

½ pound ground chuck or lamb

2 cloves garlic, chopped

1 teaspoon salt

½ teaspoon Arabian Spice (page 22)

1 (8-ounce) can tomato sauce

Preparation

Peel the zucchini and cut the ends off. Cut each in half crosswise and core the insides, leaving a shell for stuffing. Discard the pulp. Salt the insides lightly and set aside.

In a pan, heat the oil and sauté the meat with the garlic, 1 teaspoon salt, and spice blend. When the meat is cooked, set aside to cool.

Stuff the zucchini halves with the meat mixture and arrange them in a deep pan. Mix the tomato sauce with 2 cups of water and pour over the zucchini. Cover the pan and bring to a boil. Reduce the heat and simmer for 30 minutes, or until the zucchini are cooked. (You can also bake this in a 350-degrees-F oven for 50 minutes, if you prefer.) Serve with plain white rice.

Variation: *You can use either small eggplants or green peppers in place of the zucchini. You can also stuff all three vegetables for the same meal and cook in the same pan.*

MEATBALLS WITH POTATOES

RAS ASFOOR

We cook this dish during winter when fresh vegetables are scarce and very expensive. My mother used to fry the potatoes and then add them to the sauce. She also added fresh tomatoes to the sauce in the summer. This recipe is lighter then hers since I do not fry the potatoes, and I use canned diced tomatoes as I find they add a better flavor than the fresh tomatoes.

Ingredients

1 pound ground lamb or beef

2 cloves garlic, crushed

1 teaspoon salt

1 teaspoon Arabian Spice (page 22)

3 tablespoons vegetable oil, divided

1 (8-ounce) can tomato sauce

1 (8-ounce) can diced tomatoes

3 whole cardamom pods

2 pounds potatoes, peeled and
   chopped

2 cloves garlic, sliced

1 small onion, chopped

Preparation

Combine the meat with the crushed garlic, salt, and spice blend. Form into 1-inch meatballs. Sauté meatballs in 1 tablespoon oil for 5 minutes.

Pour the tomato sauce and diced tomatoes over the meatballs. Add cardamom pods and simmer for 10 minutes. Set aside.

Sauté the potatoes in the remaining 2 tablespoons of oil. Add the sliced garlic and chopped onion and cook and stir for 5 minutes.

Add potatoes to the meatball mixture. Pour in 2 cups of water, cover and cook for 20 minutes on medium heat, until the potatoes are cooked. Check the sauce to see if it needs more salt.

Serve with plain white rice (page 121) or rice with noodles (page 122).

VEGETABLES WITH MEAT PATTIES

MAFTOOL-TAPSI KUFTA BIL KHATHRAWAT · 6 to 8 servings

This is a wonderful dish that we cook during the summer when the vegetables are in season. I usually cook this dish on top of the stove using a deep pan or an electric skillet.

Ingredients

2 small Italian eggplants

3 teaspoons salt, divided

1 pound lean ground beef or lamb

2 cloves garlic, chopped

1 teaspoon Arabian Spice (page 22)

1 green pepper, sliced

1 zucchini, peeled and sliced

1 tomato, sliced

1 onion, sliced

⅓ cup olive oil

1 (8-ounce) can diced tomatoes

1 (8-ounce) can tomato sauce

Preparation

Cut the stems off the eggplants and peel off ½-inch-wide lengthwise stripes of the skin. Cut the eggplants into 1-inch thick round slices. Place the slices in a colander and sprinkle with 2 teaspoons of salt. Leave to drain in a sink for 30 minutes.

In a bowl, combine the meat with the garlic, remaining 1 teaspoon of salt, and spice blend. Make small patties, 1-inch in diameter, and set aside.

In a deep sauté pan, arrange the vegetable slices side by side, alternating with the meat patties. Drizzle olive oil over the vegetables. Pour the diced tomatoes and tomato sauce over all. Add 1 cup of water and bring to a boil. Reduce the heat and simmer, covered, for 30 minutes, until vegetables are cooked. Serve with plain white rice.

Variation: You can also bake this dish in the oven. Arrange the vegetables and meat patties in a deep baking dish side by side. Pour on the olive oil, diced tomatoes, tomato sauce, and water and cover the pan with foil. Bake in a 375-degree-F oven for 45 minutes.

VEGETABLES STUFFED WITH MEAT AND RICE

DOLMA (YAPRAGH)

6 to 8 servings

Make sure not to over stuff the vegetables with the filling in order to allow room for the rice grains to expand while cooking. Otherwise the vegetables will burst or the rice grains will not fully cook. If you are using fresh grape leaves, put them in boiling water to soften them for 5 minutes before filling them.

Ingredients

Vegetables:

3 zucchinis, peeled, cut in a half crosswise

3 small eggplants, cut in a half crosswise

2 medium onions

2 green peppers, tops cut off and seeds removed

2 tomatoes, tops cut off and cored

1 teaspoon salt

1 (16-ounce) jar grape leaves

Filling:

1 pound ground lamb or beef

1 cup white rice

1 small onion, chopped

½ cup lemon juice

Preparation

Remove enough flesh from the middle of the zucchini and eggplant halves to allow for stuffing. Salt the insides of the vegetables with 1 teaspoon of salt, and place in a colander to drain for 30 minutes.

Cut off the ends of the onions and make a cut to the center of the onion, but do not cut in a half. Place the onions in boiling water for 15 minutes. Remove from the water and separate the onion layers for stuffing.

Make the filling: Combine the meat, rice, chopped onion, lemon juice, ½ cup tomato sauce, garlic, salt, and spice blend.

Stuff each vegetable with 2 tablespoons of the filling and arrange in a deep pot. To stuff grape leaves, place 1 tablespoon of the filling in the center of a leaf. Fold the leaf over the filling and fold the sides towards the center of

(Ingredients and Preparation continued on next page)

VEGETABLES STUFFED WITH MEAT AND RICE

(CONTINUED)

1 cup tomato sauce, divided

3 cloves garlic, crushed

1 teaspoon salt

1 teaspoon Arabian Spice (page 22)

the leaf. Roll the leaf loosely and place seam down on top of the vegetables. Repeat with the rest of leaves

Stir together 1½ cups water and the remaining ½ cup tomato sauce and pour over the stuffed vegetables. Place a heatproof plate on top of the vegetables to keep them submerged. Bring to a boil over medium heat, cover and cook for 40 minutes or until rice is cooked.

To serve, cover the pot with a tray and flip the pot over onto the tray and remove. Serve with *tannour* bread and Yogurt Cucumber Salad (page 114).

MEAT AND GREEN BEAN STEW

FASULIA KHATHRA

6 servings

You can use fresh or frozen green beans for this stew. If you are using fresh beans, make sure to cut off the ends and cut each bean into 2 or 3 parts. If you are using lamb shoulder steak, trim off the fat, and keep the bones attached to the steak.

Ingredients

2 tablespoons oil

1 pound shoulder lamb steak or
  stewing beef

1 medium onion, sliced

2 cloves garlic, chopped

1 teaspoon salt

1 teaspoon Arabian Spice (page 22)

1 (8-ounce) can tomato sauce

1 pound fresh or frozen French-cut
  green beans

Preparation

In a pot, heat the oil and sauté the lamb steaks or beef chunks on both sides. Add 4 cups of water, cover, and bring to a boil. Reduce heat and simmer for 40 minutes, until the lamb or beef is tender.

Add the onion, garlic, salt, and spice blend. Pour the tomato sauce over the meat and bring to a boil. Add the green beans and simmer, covered, for 20 minutes until the green beans are tender. Adjust the salt and spices. Serve with plain white rice.

CAULIFLOWER WITH BEEF
QARNABEET BIL QEEMA

6 servings

Cauliflower is a winter vegetable. Here we chop it and add it to a meat qeema mixture. You can add 1 cup of tomato sauce to the mixture if you like.

Ingredients

2 tablespoons oil

½ pound ground chuck

1 onion, chopped

1 teaspoon salt

½ teaspoon Arabian Spice (page 22)

1 head cauliflower, chopped

¼ cup lemon juice

Preparation

Heat oil in a pan and sauté meat with onions, salt, and spice blend for 10 minutes, uncovered.

Add the chopped cauliflower and ½ cup of water. Cook for 10 minutes. When tender, add lemon juice. Simmer for 10 more minutes. Serve with white rice.

STUFFED TURNIPS

SHALGHAM MAHSHI

Turnips are root vegetables. We buy turnips with the green tops attached to ensure freshness. You can use the green tops as well as the roots. Simply sauté them in oil and garlic and add lemon juice at the end to make a delicious side dish. You can also add the green tops to soups. In this recipe, we are just using the root.

Ingredients

6 medium turnips

1 tablespoon oil

½ pound ground chuck

1 medium onion, chopped

1 tablespoon salt

1 teaspoon Arabian Spice (page 22)

1 (16-ounce) can tomato sauce, divided

1 tablespoon sugar

Juice of 1 lemon

Variation: For an easier version of this recipe, you can chop the turnips and cook them with the meat sauce.

Preparation

Wash and peel the turnips. Cut off both ends and core them to make room for filling. Place turnips in a pan with water to cover and boil for 10 minutes. Remove from heat, drain, and set aside.

In a pan, heat oil and sauté meat with onion until meat is browned. Season with salt and spice blend. Add 1 cup of the tomato sauce and cook for 10 minutes.

Arrange turnips in a deep pot. Fill turnips with meat filling and place a dessert plate over them to keep them submerged. Mix 1 cup of water, the remaining tomato sauce, sugar, and lemon juice. Pour over turnips. Simmer, covered, for 20 minutes.

Taste to see if it needs salt. Serve with white rice.

EGGPLANT CASSEROLE

TAPSI BADINJAN

Tapsi *is a term we use for all the dishes baked in a pan in the oven. When this dish is cooked in a pan (*tawa*) on top of the stove, it is called* Tawat Badinjan.

Ingredients

2 medium eggplants (about 3 pounds)

Coarse salt

½ cup corn oil

1 pound ground chuck

1 large onion, chopped

½ tablespoon Arabian Spice (page 22)

1 large onion, sliced

1 large tomato, sliced

1 (8-ounce) can tomato sauce

Preparation

Slice eggplants ½-inch thick and sprinkle with coarse salt. Put in a colander to drain for about 30 minutes. Dry eggplant slices with paper towel. Fry the slices and set aside. (Or you can place them on a baking pan, brush them with oil and put them under the broiler for 10 minutes. Flip them, and broil the other side, too.)

Preheat oven to 375 degrees F. Heat oil in a skillet and sauté the ground chuck until brown. Add the chopped onion, some salt, and the spice blend. Cook for 10 minutes.

Arrange a layer of sliced onions in bottom of a deep baking dish. Cover with sliced tomatoes. Place a layer of half of the eggplant slices. Spread the meat mixture on top. Add another layer of eggplant slices. Pour on the tomato sauce. Pour ½ cup of water on top. Cover with foil and bake for 40 minutes. Serve with white rice.

Lamb Shank and Potato Stew

LAMB, BEEF
&
POULTRY

Lamb & Beef

In Iraq, lamb is consumed more often than beef. We prepare lamb in many different ways, and use every part of the lamb, including organ meats. We cut it in chunks and cook it with vegetables as stews served with rice. We grill it as kababs, and we grind it for *kofta*, *kibbi*, and other dishes. Roasted whole baby lamb (*qousi*), prepared by slowly cooking the entire lamb in a commercial oven or a deep pit oven, is one of the most succulent dishes on the Iraqi menu. Beef may be substituted in some recipes using lamb since it is less expensive. Note that people in the Middle East prefer their meat well done.

Poultry

Poultry farming in Iraq is mostly in rural areas. When we were growing up, we purchased live chickens and slaughtered them at home. We plucked their feathers and cleaned the inside. The chickens were thin and not impressive in weight. They were free-range raised chickens and full of flavor, but very tough and needed a long time to cook.

Currently, domestic production in Iraq cannot compete with the frozen imported chickens due to the high prices of the domestic chickens. Poultry farming is inefficient and cannot satisfy the demand due to the lack of electricity, chicken feed, and veterinary care that resulted in the decline of domestic chicken farming.

We usually boil chicken with whole aromatic spices, and then use the broth to cook bulgur and rice. Sometimes we cook chicken in tomato sauce and add rice or bulgur to it when the chicken is half-way cooked and simmer together. This makes a complete meal with salads and pickles on the side.

Sometimes we make chicken stew in tomato sauce with potatoes or peas. We serve it with plain white rice. We also make chicken soup with rice or chickpeas, and serve it with bread. You can find these recipes in the grains and soup sections of this book.

ROASTED WHOLE LAMB

QOUSI

15 to 20 servings

This is a meal that we prepare during both celebrations and mourning because it easily feeds a large gathering. It is the ultimate homage to our guests. A large tray of rice with a whole lamb on top is rather expensive, but serves a lot of people. Guests either serve themselves on plates or stand around the communal tray and use the three fingers of their right hands to pick on the lamb and scoop the rice on their side of the tray. Typically we stuff the lamb with cooked rice, raisins, almonds, and meat qeema. Sometimes, however, we do not stuff it and instead serve it over a tray of rice. We usually take the lamb to the public bakery to slowly bake it in their large brick oven for a few hours. Sometimes we order the whole lamb from a specialized restaurant that delivers the cooked lamb on a big tray of rice for the party.

Ingredients

1 20-pound whole lamb

6 cinnamon sticks

1 tablespoon whole allspice

1 tablespoon whole cloves

Spice Paste:

4 tablespoons Arabian Spice
  (page 22)

4 tablespoons salt

10 cloves garlic, chopped

1 cup tomato paste

½ cup vegetable oil

Note: For this recipe, you need to order a small 20-pound lamb from the butcher—make sure your oven is big enough! If it's not you can use 3 legs of lamb instead of the whole lamb.

Preparation

Preheat oven to 350 degrees F. Rinse the lamb and dry it with paper towels. Place the lamb in a deep roasting pan.

In a bowl, mix all the spice paste ingredients to make a paste. Coat the lamb with the spice paste. Pour 6 cups of water into the pan. Put the cinnamon sticks, whole allspice and cloves in the pan for an aromatic flavor.

Cover the lamb with foil and bake in the oven for 6 to 7 hours. When the meat falls off the bone, then you know it is done. (In Iraq, we usually cook it well done.)

Serve it with white or saffron rice with peas. Decorate with fried potatoes and sliced hard-boiled eggs. You can also decorate the rice with Almond and Raisin Dressing (page 132).

BRAISED LEG OF LAMB

FAKHID MISHWI

4 to 6 servings

My sister Samar cooks this recipe on top of the stove instead of in the oven. She serves the lamb on a bed of rice and garnishes it with sliced hard-boiled eggs, toasted almonds, and raisins.

Ingredients

1 (8-pound) leg of lamb

1 tablespoon Arabian Spice (page 22)

1 teaspoon salt

4 whole cinnamon sticks

4 whole cardamom pods

4 whole allspice

4 whole cloves

½ pound pearl onions, peeled

2 large potatoes, peeled and sliced

Toasted almonds and golden raisins
    for decoration

Ground cinnamon

Cooked plain white rice (page 121)

3 hard-boiled eggs, peeled and sliced

Preparation

Place the leg of lamb in a big pot. Sear the lamb for a few minutes on each side until lightly browned. Season it with the spice blend and salt. Pour 3 to 4 cups of water into the pan and add the whole spices.

Cover the pot and leave it to cook on medium-low heat for 3 to 4 hours on top of the stove, turning the leg of lamb once halfway through.

Add the pearl onions and sliced potatoes towards the end to cook with the lamb (or you could fry the potatoes separately and decorate the rice with them).

In a pan, sauté the almonds in a little oil for 3 minutes. When toasted, add the golden raisins and sauté for 1 minute. Remove from the pan immediately to a plate to prevent them from burning. Sprinkle ground cinnamon over them.

To serve, place the rice on a large platter, top with the toasted almond and raisin mixture and the egg slices. Then top with the potatoes. Place leg of lamb on top of all and serve juices from the pan on the side.

ROASTED LEG OF LAMB

FAKHID MISHWI BIL FIRIN

6 servings

I very much enjoy preparing this dish. The aroma of whole spices fills the kitchen as you bake it in the oven and the enticing scents of garlic, cinnamon, and cloves burst forth as you slice the leg of lamb.

Ingredients

1 (8-pound) leg of lamb

6 cloves garlic

4 whole cloves

4 whole allspice

2 cinnamon sticks

4 whole cardamom pods

1 tablespoon curry powder

1 tablespoon salt

2 large onions, sliced

2 pounds potatoes, peeled and sliced

Preparation

Preheat oven to 375 degrees F.

Poke the leg of lamb all over with a knife and fill the holes with the garlic and whole spices. (Break cinnamon sticks into small pieces.) Rub the lamb with curry powder and salt.

Line a large roasting pan with foil. Place the lamb on it and cover with slices of onion. Arrange potatoes around the lamb and seal pan with foil. Place the pan in the oven and roast the lamb for 2 hours.

To serve, place the lamb on a platter and surround it with the potatoes and lamb drippings. Serve with white or saffron rice and decorate with almonds and raisins.

LEG OF LAMB WITH TOMATOES

DOUB

6 servings

I usually cook this recipe in a pressure cooker to save time. You can also put the leg of lamb in a deep pot and cook it on top of the stove for 3 hours on low heat.

Ingredients

1 (8-pound) leg of lamb

1 tablespoon oil

1 (8-ounce) can tomato sauce

1 (32-ounce) can diced tomatoes

5 cloves garlic, sliced

6 whole cardamom pods

1 cinnamon stick

1 teaspoon whole allspice

 4 whole cloves

1 teaspoon salt

2 pounds potatoes, peeled and cubed

Preparation

Put the leg of lamb into a pressure cooker and sauté in oil for 5 minutes on each side to brown. Add 3 cups of water, the tomato sauce, diced tomatoes, garlic, whole spices, and salt. Cover and cook on medium heat for 40 minutes. Remove from heat and leave the pot to cool to release the pressure.

Add the potatoes to the meat and cook in the sauce for 20 minutes on medium heat or until soft, adding more water if needed. (When you add potatoes to the sauce cover the pot with a plate and not the pressure cooker's cover.) Serve with white or saffron rice.

SHISH KABABS

KUFTA KABAB

8 servings

The term kufta *means ground beef or lamb shaped into meat patties or formed around skewers* (sheesh) *like a sausage. To prepare this dish, you need eight flat metal skewers. If you use bamboo skewers, you need to soak them in water for one hour to prevent them from burning while under the broiler or on the grill. There are many variations to this recipe, but the most common recipe ingredients are meat, onions, and salt. The following recipe is my mother's.*

Ingredients

1 pound ground lamb

1 small onion, chopped

1 clove garlic, chopped

1 pound ground beef

3 tablespoons flour

1 tablespoon salt

1 teaspoon Arabian Spice (page 22)

Tannour bread for serving

Ground summac for sprinkling

Preparation

Prepare a charcoal grill if you are grilling outdoors; otherwise turn the broiler on to 400 degrees F.

Place lamb, chopped onions, and garlic in the food processor and pulse it eight times. Take the mixture out of the food processor and put in a bowl. Add the beef, flour, salt, and spice blend, and knead it by hand until the mixture is well blended. Cover and refrigerate for 30 minutes.

Have a bowl of cold water nearby to wet your hands while forming the kababs. Divide the meat into 8 large meatballs. Hold a skewer in one hand and with the other hand insert one of the meatballs onto the skewer and shape it into a sausage around the skewer. Press firmly and make the meat about 8 to 9 inches long. Repeat with remaining meatballs.

Place the skewers on a charcoal grill about 5 inches above the coals. (If you are grilling under the broiler in the oven, make sure to place the tray on the top rack 5 inches below the broiler.) Grill for 5 minutes on each side.

When kababs are cooked through and nicely browned, slip them off the skewers to a plate lined with *tannour* bread (*khubz*). Sprinkle summac over them and cover with another piece of bread to keep them warm.

Serve this dish with Arabic Salad (page 105), Onion and Summac Salad (page 113), parsley, basil (*reehan*), and pickles (*turshi*).

Grilling kebabs at an outdoor picnic

Muslim families buy sheep to be slaughtered by a butcher to prepare it for the celebration of the Feast of Sacrifice (*Ied Al Athha*). The butcher performs the ritual slaughter in the backyard of the family home and cuts the animal into pieces for cooking. He carefully removes the organ meat to be grilled. The intestines, stomach, feet, and head are for the *Pacha* dish (page 218). It is considered sacrilege to throw away any meat. Sometimes, they sacrifice a lamb and distribute the meat to neighbors or take it to the mosque when the family's wish for healing, a wedding, success, or a newborn baby boy is granted (*Nither*).

The most common type of sheep in Iraq is the fat-tailed sheep called the *Awassi* after the name of a tribe called Al-Awas who occupy the land between the Tigris and the Euphrates rivers. Two other varieties of sheep are the *N'eimi* and the *Shafali* that graze on lowlands and are named after tribes also. They are all distinctive in having lean meat with their fat stored in the tail. Because of this, when we grill *tekka*, we insert pieces of fat between the pieces of lamb on the skewers to prevent the meat from drying out on the grill.

CHAR-GRILLED LAMB KABABS

TEKKA

6 to 8 servings

Tekka is tender lamb cubes grilled on skewers on a charcoal grill called a manqal *and served in* sammoun *bread or tannour bread with sliced tomatoes, sliced onions, and parsley. Tekka is a popular street food sandwich that you can find throughout the cities and while you travel in the countryside too. It is also prepared outdoors during family picnics. Iraqi lamb is very sweet and tender and does not need a long time to cook.*

Ingredients

6 pounds lamb cubes

1 teaspoon salt

1 teaspoon Arabian Spice (page 22)

6 metal skewers

Sammoun or *tannour* bread

Onion slices

Tomato slices

Parsley

Preparation

Place the lamb in a bowl and sprinkle with the salt and spice blend and mix well. Place in the refrigerator for 30 minutes.

Take meat out of the refrigerator and slide the lamb cubes onto skewers. Arrange them on a charcoal grill about 5 inches above the coals and grill for 8 minutes, turning the skewers frequently.

Serve the meat while still on a skewer or pull the skewer out and slide the meat inside *sammoun* or *tannour* bread with sliced onion, sliced tomatoes, and parsley.

Variation: You can alternate chunks of lamb on the skewer with onions, tomatoes, and green peppers, if you prefer.

LAMB SHANK AND POTATO STEW

MARAQAT LAHAM / MURQAT LAHAM

6 servings

This is a very popular stew served over rice. Many of the roadside cafes serve it to their customers as the dish of the day.

Ingredients

¼ cup oil

3 pounds lamb shanks or stewing lamb

1 teaspoon ground cardamom

1 cinnamon stick

5 whole cloves

5 whole allspice

½ teaspoon Arabian Spice (page 22)

1 small onion, chopped

3 cloves garlic, chopped

1 teaspoon salt

3 tablespoons tomato paste

2 large potatoes, quartered

Preparation

Heat the oil in a large pot. Sauté the lamb in oil for 5 minutes to brown. Add the spices, onion, garlic, and salt and cook for 5 minutes.

Add 4 cups of water and the tomato paste and bring to a boil. Reduce heat and simmer the lamb, covered, for 90 minutes or more, until the meat is tender.

Add the potatoes and cook for 20 more minutes, until the potatoes are cooked. Skim off the fat.

Serve with *tannour* bread in a soup bowl, or over plain white rice.

(See photo, page 204)

TRIPE, INTESTINES, SHEEP'S HEAD AND FEET
PACHA

As a child, I remember how we received the tripe from the butcher un-bleached. My mother, aunt, and grandma spent hours in the kitchen scraping the tripe with the back of a knife and hooking the lamb intestines to the water tap to clean the inside of the intestines. They removed most of the fat attached to the intestines before turning the intestines inside out. To sanitize the intestines and the tripe, they covered them with salt, vinegar, lemon juice, and 1 cup of flour, and let them soak for a few hours. They then washed them thoroughly. When the tripe and intestines smelled clean, they stuffed them. They cut the tripe in 4 by 6 inch pieces and sewed them together to make a pouch. They stuffed the pouches (*keepayat, kirsha*) until half full, and then sewed the opening half shut.

There are many restaurants in Iraq that specialize in *pacha*, a dish that requires about 8 hours of slow-cooking these stuffed lamb parts in a 36-inch diameter pot. The pot contains the stuffed tripe, stuffed intestines, lamb's head, lamb's feet, and tongue. They serve this dish in a big soup bowl with a little of everything along with *tannour* bread and slices of lemon and onions on the side. The restaurants usually give instructions to the adventurous on how to eat this meal. You are supposed to remove the thread of the tripe pouch and drop the filling in the soup to absorb the flavors and moisten the filling. You also put slices of bread in the soup bowl and squeeze some lemon over the soup. These restaurants are open very late at night and very early in the morning as this soup is supposed to cure hangovers.

There are many Assyrian and Chaldean restaurants in Chicago, Detroit, and other cities worldwide that cater to *pacha* fans, and they often make it the special for the day.

(See pages 218-219 for my recipe for *pacha* that you can make at home.)

STUFFED TRIPE AND LAMB CASINGS

HASHWAT KEEPAYAT AND BANABEERS—PACHA

10 to 12 servings

Ingredients

2 cups white rice or medium grain
   bulgur, rinsed and drained

10 cloves garlic, minced

1 large onion, chopped

2 pounds chopped lamb

1 tablespoon salt

1 tablespoon Arabian Spice (page 22)

4 pounds lamb tripe

10 feet lamb casing from butcher

Preparation

Make the stuffing: Combine the rice, garlic, onion, chopped lamb, salt, and spice blend in a bowl. Set aside.

Cut the tripe into 4 by 6 inch pieces (about 6 to 8), and sew the pieces into pouches leaving an opening for stuffing. Stuff the tripe pouches half full with the stuffing and sew the openings shut. (Make sure to use cotton string to sew the pouches.)

Stuff the lamb casings lightly with the stuffing. Do not overstuff or they will burst when the rice expands during the cooking process. You can cut the casings in 1-foot-long pieces and tie the ends with a string before you drop them in the soup.

Cook the stuffed tripe and stuffed lamb casings in the soup base. (See recipe opposite page.)

STUFFED TRIPE AND LAMB CASING SOUP

BANABEER

Ingredients

2 teaspoons salt

2 cups dry chickpeas, soaked
   overnight in water

2 large onions, sliced

1 pound soup bones

Stuffed lamb casings and tripe
   (opposite page)

Toasted pita bread

Lemon slices

Preparation

Place all of the ingredients except the lamb casings and tripe and pita bread in a large pot with 15 cups of water. Bring to a boil and cook for 40 minutes. Remove from heat and cool for 30 minutes.

Add 2 cups of ice water to cool the soup and then add the stuffed casings and tripe. (If you add the casings while the soup is boiling, they will shrink.) Bring to a boil, and then reduce heat to medium and cook for 2 to 3 hours.

To serve, place toasted bread in soup bowls and ladle the soup and the casings and tripe into soup bowls. Serve lemon slices on the side.

CURRIES

In the beginning of the eighteenth century, the Ottoman sultan created the Mamluk army in Iraq. They took control of Baghdad and the southern cities and controlled the floodplain from Kurdistan in the north to the Persian Gulf in the south. It was a time of recovery and redevelopment in Iraq. The Ottoman rulers established the canal system, education, and government.

The Mamluks allowed the British East India Company to establish a trading post in Basra in 1763, and that was the beginning of the British influence and later domination of Iraq. Indian tea and spices began to make their way through the waterways from Basra to the northern cities. Curry became an ingredient used in many recipes in the south of Iraq rather than the Kurdish areas of the north. Many Iraqis began to cook chicken and lamb curry stews and serve them with plain white rice and bread on the side.

BEEF OR LAMB CURRY

KARI BIL LAHAM

4 servings

In Iraq we usually purchase the curry spice mixture from the spice market. You can add chili powder to the mixture if you prefer a hot and spicy flavor. I usually purchase mild curry and then add the chili later so I can control the heat. I prefer to use lamb for this recipe since it cooks faster and is easier for digestion.

Ingredients

⅓ cup vegetable oil

1 large onion, chopped

4 cloves garlic, chopped

3 tablespoons curry powder

1 teaspoon salt

2 pounds stewing beef or lamb

3 tablespoons tomato paste

1 cup diced tomatoes

2 large potatoes, cut in 1-inch cubes

Preparation

Heat the oil in a saucepan. Add the onion and garlic and sauté until soft. Stir in the curry powder and salt and cook for a minute or two. Add the meat and sauté for 10 minutes, browning on all sides.

Dilute the tomato paste in 1 cup of water and pour over the meat. Add the diced tomatoes and 2 cups of water and bring to a boil. Reduce the heat and simmer the meat for 1 hour.

When the meat is cooked and tender, add the potatoes and a little more water if needed. Cook, covered, for 20 more minutes, until the potatoes are soft.

Serve with plain white rice, Yogurt Drink (page 63), Arabic Salad (page 105), and bread.

CHICKEN CURRY

DIJAJ BIL KARI

I always use chicken with the skin and bones to give better flavor to the sauce. Skim off the fat and remove the skin when the chicken is cooked.

Ingredients

⅓ cup vegetable oil

1 large onion, sliced

4 cloves garlic, sliced

3 tablespoons curry powder

1 teaspoon salt

3 pounds chicken pieces with skin and bones

1 cup diced tomatoes

1 cup tomato sauce

2 large potatoes, peeled and sliced

Preparation

Heat the oil in a saucepan. Add the onion and garlic and sauté until soft. Stir in the curry powder and salt and cook for a few minutes. Add the chicken pieces and sauté them for 10 minutes, browning on both sides.

Add the diced tomatoes, tomato sauce, and 2 cups of water and bring to a boil. Reduce heat and simmer the chicken, covered, for 10 minutes.

Remove the chicken skins and skim off the fat. Add the potatoes and cook for 20 more minutes until the potatoes are soft. Serve with plain white rice.

Variation: You can add 1 cup of frozen peas to the sauce at the end and cook for 10 minutes longer.

CHICKEN WITH RICE STUFFING

DIJAJ MAHSHI

4 servings

This is a very festive meal served for special guests or during the holidays. You use the same stuffing as for the stuffed turkey recipe (see page 227). Serve any leftover rice dressing as a side dish.

Ingredients

1 (3-pound) whole chicken

Rice Stuffing (page 227)

3 tablespoons vegetable oil

3 tablespoons tomato paste

1 can (8-ounce) tomato sauce

1 medium onion, chopped

2 cloves garlic, chopped

1 whole cinnamon stick

4 whole cardamom pods

1 teaspoon salt

1 pound fresh or frozen peas

Preparation

Wash the chicken and remove the fat from cavity. Fill the cavity with the rice stuffing. Sew the cavity closed with butcher yarn.

Heat vegetable oil in a deep pot and sauté the chicken on all sides until the skin is lightly browned. Add the tomato paste, tomato sauce, onion, garlic, and 3 cups of water and bring to a boil. Add the whole spices and salt.

Cover the pot and simmer for 45 minutes. When the chicken is cooked, add the peas and cook for 15 more minutes.

Remove the chicken to a platter with a bed of white rice. Pour the sauce in a deep bowl to serve with the chicken and stuffing.

CHICKEN WITH BULGUR STUFFING

HASHWAT BULGUR

4 servings

Bulgur stuffing is very common in Mosul and northern parts of Iraq since wheat grows in the north, and bulgur is consumed there daily. When cooking bulgur pilaf, we usually use no. 3 or no. 4 coarse grain of bulgur.

Ingredients

1 (3-pound) whole chicken
3 tablespoons vegetable oil
3 tablespoons tomato paste
1 can (8-ounce) tomato sauce
1 medium onion, chopped
2 cloves garlic, chopped
1 whole cinnamon stick
4 whole cardamom pods
1 teaspoon salt
1 pound fresh or frozen peas

Bulgur stuffing:
Liver and heart of chicken, chopped
1 tablespoon butter
1 small onion, chopped
1 teaspoon salt
1 teaspoon Arabian Spice (page 22)
1½ cups chicken stock or water
1 cup coarse bulgur
½ cup frozen peas

Preparation

Make the bulgur stuffing:
Sauté the heart and liver in butter in a skillet. Add onion, salt, and spice blend, and cook for 5 minutes. Add the stock and bulgur and bring to a boil. Add peas and reduce heat to simmer for 20 minutes, until stock is absorbed and bulgur is tender. Fluff the pilaf using a spoon and uncover to allow to cool.

Wash the chicken and remove the fat from cavity. Fill the cavity with the bulgur stuffing. Sew the cavity closed with butcher yarn.

Heat vegetable oil in a deep pot and sauté the chicken on all sides until the skin is lightly browned. Add the tomato paste, tomato sauce, onion, garlic, and 3 cups of water and bring to a boil. Add the whole spices and salt. Cover the pot and simmer for 45 minutes.

When the chicken is cooked, add the peas and cook for 15 more minutes. Remove the chicken to a platter with a bed of white rice. Pour the sauce in a deep bowl to serve with the chicken and bulgur stuffing.

CHICKEN WITH POTATOES

TEPSI DIJAJ BIL BATATA

4 to 6 servings

Baking chicken in the oven is not common in Iraq. We usually cook meals on top of the stove. But I find it easy to assemble this dish and bake it in the oven while I prepare the vegetables and rice on top of the stove.

Ingredients

1 large onion, sliced

1 whole chicken, cut up

1 teaspoon salt

1 teaspoon ground coriander

2 cloves garlic, sliced

1 (8-ounce) can diced tomatoes

1 cinnamon stick

5 whole cardamom pods

3 large potatoes, sliced

1 (8-ounce) can tomato sauce

Preparation

Preheat oven to 350 degrees F. Arrange the onions on the bottom of a deep baking pan.

Put chicken in a bowl and season with the salt and coriander. Arrange chicken pieces on top of the onions along with the garlic. Pour the diced tomatoes on top of the chicken. Tuck the whole spices under the chicken pieces. Arrange potato slices around the chicken pieces.

Mix the tomato sauce with 2 cups of water and pour over the chicken. Cover with foil and bake for 1 hour. Serve with rice.

TURKEY WITH RICE STUFFING

ALI SHISH

6 to 8 servings

When I was growing up in Iraq, we used to purchase the turkey alive, and then slaughter it, clean it, and cook it for our New Year's Eve dinner. Imported frozen turkey and chicken became available in the 1970s and we started buying cases of frozen poultry and keeping them in the freezer for later use. For this recipe, buy a small fresh turkey.

Ingredients

Rice Stuffing:

3 teaspoons oil, divided

½ pound ground chuck or lamb

1 small onion, chopped

1 teaspoon salt

1 teaspoon Arabian Spice (page 22)

½ cup slivered almonds

½ cup raisins

2 cups cooked rice

Turkey:

1 8- to 10-pound turkey

2 tablespoons oil

1 large onion, sliced

1 (6-ounce) can tomato paste

1 cinnamon stick

5 whole cloves

5 whole cardamoms

5 whole allspice

1 tablespoon salt

3 large potatoes, peeled and cubed
   (optional)

Preparation

Rice stuffing:
In a pan, heat 2 teaspoons of oil and sauté meat until browned. Add the onion, salt, and spice blend and stir. In a separate pan sauté almonds in 1 teaspoon of oil until toasted. Add raisins and stir for 1 more minute. Add to the meat along with the cooked rice and stir to combine. Set aside to cool.

Turkey:
Rinse the turkey and stuff the cavity with the cooled meat and rice stuffing. Sew the cavity closed. In a large pot, heat oil and sauté turkey for 10 minutes browning on all sides. Add 10 cups of water, onion, tomato paste, whole spices, and salt. Cover and cook on top of the stove over medium heat for 3 hours or until turkey is cooked. Add potatoes during the last 30 minutes if desired.

Serve turkey on a deep dish with Saffron Rice (page 123) and Arabic Salad (page 105).

FISH

Fish

Fish (*samak*) was an important part of the ancient Iraqi diet. There were over 50 types of fish mentioned in the Sumerian tablets. The Mesopotamian marshlands (Al Ahwar) of southern Iraq are part of the Tigris and Euphrates basin. Some 106 species of freshwater fish have been recorded there. The most favored species are called *Gattan*, *Shabout*, *Bunni*, *Biz*, and *Zubaidi*, caught in the Tigris or Euphrates rivers or raised in fish farms. Southern marshes were drained in 1991 during the reign of Saddam Hussein to quell the revolt of the Shias against the regime. The inhabitants were displaced and the ecosystem was devastated. Presently, the U.S. and the Iraqi government are working on rebuilding the marshes and revitalizing the fish industry in the wetlands.

FISH WITH RICE
SIMACH UMTABAQ

6 to 8 servings

When my sister Maysoon came to visit me, she made this dish that originated in Basra in the southern part of Iraq. Traditionally, the fish is fried and then layered with the cooked rice. Here you broil the fish after covering it with a spice rub.

Ingredients

3 pounds boneless, skinless filets of
   tilapia or flounder
Vegetable oil
3 large onions, sliced
2 tablespoons crushed dried lime
   (*noomi Basra*)
4 cups cooked plain white rice

Spice Rub:
1 tablespoon salt
3 tablespoons ground coriander
2 tablespoons curry powder
3 tablespoons crushed dried lime
   (*noomi Basra*)
4 cloves garlic, pressed

Preparation

In a small bowl, combine all the ingredients for the spice rub. Rub on fish filets and marinate in the refrigerator for 6 hours.

Heat oil in a large skillet and deep fry the onions until they become light brown in color; drain on paper towels.

Line a baking sheet with foil. Drizzle some vegetable oil on the foil and lay the fish filets on top. Drizzle some oil over the fish. Place the baking sheet under the broiler for 10 minutes. Turn off the heat and place the fish in the middle rack of the oven for 5 more minutes to finish cooking. Remove from oven.

Preheat oven to 375 degrees F. Arrange a layer of half of the onions on the bottom of a deep pan. Place half the fish on top and sprinkle with 1 tablespoon of crushed dried lime. Spread 2 cups of cooked rice on top. Repeat layers of onions, fish, dried lime, and rice. Cover with foil and bake for 30 minutes.

Remove the pot from the oven and leave on the kitchen counter to set for 15 minutes. Remove the foil and place a tray or a deep dish on top of the pot and flip the pot upside down and remove. Serve this dish with pickles and Arabic Salad (page 105).

Masgoof fish being grilled
around an open fire

GRILLED WHOLE FISH

SAMAK MASGOOF

Masgoof *is not a type of fish; rather it is the method by which the fish is cooked. You can use trout, blue fish, or carp for this recipe. The fish is cut open along the spine, washed, and sprinkled with salt. Each fish is skewered and placed next to an open fire to cook slowly for 45 minutes until golden brown. Some people have a tannour oven built in their backyard for bread baking, and they also use it to grill fish and chicken. They lay the fish in a long metal basket, close the basket, and secure the handle with a lock to keep the fish from falling out. They then slide the basket into the tannour and turn the fish a few times until roasted and thoroughly cooked. To cook masgoof in your home, use the oven and follow this recipe.*

Ingredients

1 tablespoon salt

1 tablespoon curry powder

3 tablespoons tomato paste

½ cup lemon juice

5 cloves garlic, crushed

½ cup vegetable oil

1 (10-pound) whole trout or blue fish

Preparation

Combine all the ingredients except the fish in a bowl and mix well to blend the spices and make a paste. Preheat oven to 350 degrees F.

Cut the fish along the spine. Do not remove the scales of the fish. Wash it and leave it in a colander in the sink to drain for 15 minutes.

Remove the fish from the colander and place it on a foil-lined baking pan. Cover the fish with the prepared paste. Bake the fish for 40 minutes, or until cooked.

Serve with plain white rice and salad.

Variations: You can cook an Herb Sauce (page 235) for the fish as a side dish to go with the rice.

In Mosul, we cover the fish with the Herb Sauce when the fish is halfway cooked and put it back in the oven to finish cooking. This way, the fish will absorb the flavors from the sauce.

BROILED FISH

SAMAK MISHWI

4 servings

For this dish, you can use tilapia or catfish. I usually rub the fish with the spice rub the day before and keep it in the refrigerator so I can broil it the next day.

Ingredients

4 pieces (about 3 pounds) fresh
   boneless, skinless fish filets (tilapia
   or catfish)
4 tablespoons vegetable oil for
   drizzling

Spice Rub:

1 tablespoon salt
3 tablespoons ground coriander
2 tablespoons curry powder
3 tablespoons crushed dried
   lime (*noomi Basra*)
4 cloves garlic, pressed

Preparation

In a small bowl, combine all the ingredients for the spice rub. Coat the fish filets with the spice rub. Place them on a tray and cover with foil. Refrigerate for at least 6 hours.

Line a baking sheet with foil. Drizzle some vegetable oil on the foil and lay the fish filets on top. Drizzle some oil over the fish. Place the baking sheet under the broiler for 10 minutes. Turn off the heat and place the fish in the middle rack of the oven for 5 more minutes to finish cooking. Serve with rice, pickles, and salads.

FISH FILETS IN HERB SAUCE

SAMAK BIL KHALTA

4 servings

You could make the herb sauce and serve it as a side dish with grilled or baked fish (page 233). You can prepare it ahead of time and freeze it, and then reheat some whenever you cook fish.

Ingredients

4 filets tilapia or flounder

Herb Sauce:
⅓ cup vegetable oil
1 large onion, chopped
4 cloves garlic, chopped
1 cup chopped scallions
1 teaspoon salt
1 tablespoon curry powder
2 large tomatoes, diced
2 cups chopped parsley
1 tablespoon tomato paste
1 tablespoon crushed dried lime
   (*noomi Basra*)
Juice of 1 lemon

Preparation

Make Herb Sauce:
Pour the oil in a deep pan and sauté the onion and garlic for 5 minutes. Add the scallions, salt, and curry powder and stir for 3 minutes. Add the tomatoes, parsley, tomato paste, and 1 cup of water and bring to a boil. Sprinkle dried lime over the sauce and add the lemon juice. Boil until the tomatoes are cooked and then reduce the heat.

Add the fish filets to the sauce and simmer, covered, for 15 minutes on low heat. To serve, ladle the sauce into a deep dish and place the fish on top of the sauce. Serve with plain white rice or saffron rice (page 123).

Sammoun Bread

BREADS

Breads

A large variety of commercially produced breads, such as *sammoun* and *tannour* breads, are available for purchase daily from the public bakeries in Iraq. You can try to make this bread at home in a conventional oven, and though they do not look the same as the professionally made ones, they still taste delicious. I developed my recipes for these breads through trial and error, and was very pleased with the eventual results.

Qosa bread and *saj* bread are specialties of Mosul and the Kurdish area of the country, and are usually baked at home. Although *saj* bread (which is similar to *lavash*) is available commercially, families usually enjoy using their special flour to make this bread.

SIMEET

Simeet *is a bread snack that we purchase from street vendors in Iraq. The vendors carry the tray stacked with* simeet *on their heads and roam the streets calling, "Simeet, Simeet." It is very similar to sesame bagels. This recipe is adapted to make it easy to prepare at home.*

Ingredients

Dough:

1 teaspoon dry yeast

1 teaspoon sugar

1¼ cups warm water

3 cups bread flour

1 teaspoon salt

1 teaspoon oil for the bowl

Topping:

2 teaspoons molasses

1 cup sesame seeds

Preparation

Dissolve yeast and sugar in ¼ cup warm water and let it stand for 5 minutes. Mix the flour and salt together. Make a well in the center. Pour the yeast mixture and remaining 1 cup of warm water into the center of the flour and mix to form a dough. Knead for 5 minutes or until dough becomes smooth and elastic. Cover the dough and leave it in a warm place to rise for 2 hours or until doubled in bulk.

Turn out the dough onto a lightly floured surface and punch down. Knead for 2 minutes. Divide into 16 pieces and shape pieces into 10-inch long ropes. Take 2 ropes and twist them together. Bring the ends together and seal to make a 4-inch-wide ring. Repeat with remaining ropes.

Pour the molasses into ½ cup of water and stir. (You could use sugar instead of molasses; sugar gives the *simeet* a toasty color.) Dip each dough ring in the molasses mixture and then in a bowl of the sesame seeds. Make sure each *simeet* is well coated with sesame seeds. Arrange on a tray covered with parchment paper. Cover the rings with a kitchen towel and leave to rise for 1 hour. Preheat oven to 450 F.

Bake the *simeets* for 20 to 25 minutes or until golden brown. Place on a wire rack to cool. Serve with tea and cheese.

I remember my late Aunt Matheela in Mosul who used to bake hundreds of these thin breads and keep them in big wooden containers in the cellar for her family for winter. Before serving the bread, they sprayed it with water to soften it and then ate it with white cheese or *tahini* and honey or *dibis*, or with dinner. When people from Mosul migrated to Baghdad, they carried on the tradition of making this bread and it was sold to the Maslawi community.

SAJ BREAD

KHUBIZ SAJ / KHUBIZ RIQAQ

Makes 10 to 15 pieces

Saj bread is baked by peasants in the villages north of Iraq. It is a thin unleavened bread and resembles lavash bread. Flat and round, it is baked on an upside-down hot iron wok surface (saj).

Ingredients

1 cup whole wheat flour

3 cups white all-purpose flour

1 teaspoon salt

1 teaspoon nigella black seeds

1½ cups warm water

Note: Today's cooks use a Chinese wok or an iron skillet to replace the *saj* by placing it over a gas or electric burner on top of the stove. You can also bake these breads on a sheet pan in a 500-degree-F oven for 2 minutes under the broiler.

Preparation

In a bowl, combine the flours, salt, and nigella seeds. Make a well in the middle and pour in the warm water and stir to combine (adjust amount of water as needed to make a smooth dough, some flours require more water). Knead the dough for 10 minutes. Cover the bowl with a towel and leave for 30 minutes to rest.

Cut the dough in small pieces the size of an egg. Arrange on a floured surface. Cover with a kitchen towel and leave to rest for 30 minutes.

Take a piece of dough and flatten it with your hand on a floured board. With a rolling pin, roll it out very thin to about 9 inches in diameter. Add more flour on the board as needed. Put the flattened dough on the hot *saj* surface (similar to an upside-down wok—see Note).

Flip the bread after 1 minute and cook the other side for another minute. Remove the bread from the *saj* when you see the bubbles formed on the surface. Repeat with remaining dough.

Arrange on a large tray to dry out before storing. You can fold each piece and stack them on top of each other, covered with a kitchen towel to keep them soft. Put them in a freezer bag and freeze them or keep in the refrigerator.

YELLOW BREAD QOSA SAFGHA **Makes 20 pieces**

This bread, a variation of qosa bread (at right), is baked during Lent and is a specialty of the Christian community of Mosul. Follow the qosa recipe but add ½ teaspoon of turmeric powder to the dough to give it the yellow color. Alternatively, you could use 1 teaspoon of saffron soaked in hot water instead of turmeric and add to the flour while kneading the dough. With this recipe, you do not brush the top with egg wash because it is consumed during Lent. Instead of balls, shape the dough in braids or coils. This design symbolizes the heads of the apostles.

SESAME BREAD

QOSA

Makes 6 to 8 pieces

There is nothing more delicious than the aroma of baking bread and the prospect of eating it warm from the oven. Qosa bread is very similar to the Italian focaccia bread. This bread is a specialty of Mosul and the Kurdish area of the country. My aunt Matheela used the tannour oven to bake them, but I have had success baking them in a conventional oven at home.

Ingredients

1 tablespoon dry yeast

1 cup warm water, divided

4½ cups all-purpose flour

1 teaspoon nigella seeds

1 teaspoon ground fennel seeds

1 teaspoon salt

⅓ cup vegetable oil

1 egg, beaten

½ cup sesame seeds

Preparation

In a bowl, dissolve yeast in ½ cup of warm water, cover, and set aside to rise for about 10 minutes.

Mix the flour, nigella seeds, ground fennel seeds, and salt. Add oil and rub mixture in your hands to mix well. Add the yeast and another ½ cup of warm water. Knead the dough for 5 minutes, adding more water or flour if needed to make a smooth dough. Brush the dough with oil. Cover it with a towel and put in a warm place to rise for 1 hour.

Uncover the dough and cut into balls the size of an orange. Arrange the dough balls on a floured surface and cover with a towel. Flatten each piece of dough with your hands and place them on a baking sheet. Cover with a towel and allow dough to rise for 45 minutes. Preheat oven to 375 degrees F.

Slash the surface of each dough disk with a diamond design. Brush the tops with the beaten egg and sprinkle sesame seeds on top. Place the baking sheet in the middle rack of the oven. Bake for 25 to 30 minutes until lightly golden. Remove from the oven and place the bread on a rack to cool. Serve with cheese and tea.

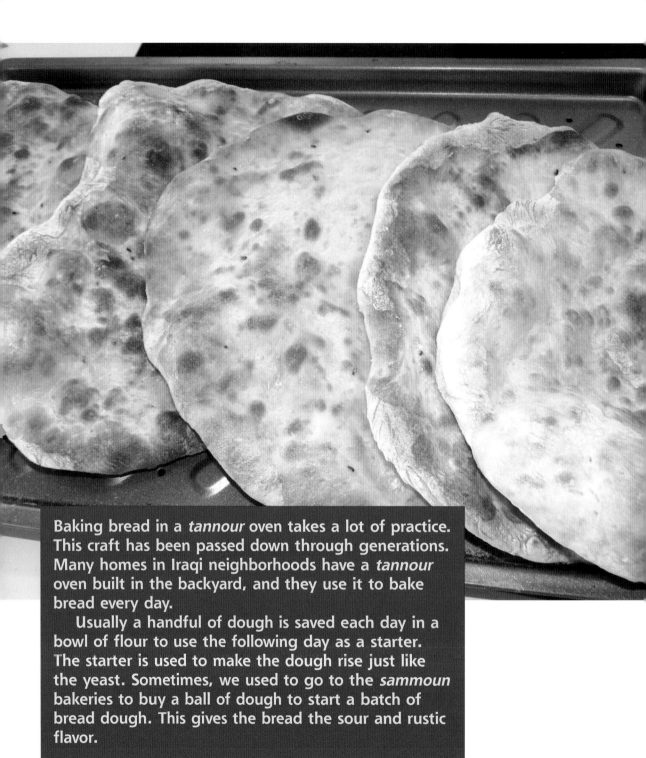

Baking bread in a *tannour* oven takes a lot of practice. This craft has been passed down through generations. Many homes in Iraqi neighborhoods have a *tannour* oven built in the backyard, and they use it to bake bread every day.

Usually a handful of dough is saved each day in a bowl of flour to use the following day as a starter. The starter is used to make the dough rise just like the yeast. Sometimes, we used to go to the *sammoun* bakeries to buy a ball of dough to start a batch of bread dough. This gives the bread the sour and rustic flavor.

TANNOUR BREAD

KHUBIZ TANNOUR

Makes 6 pieces

In Iraq, this traditional bread is purchased fresh daily from the bakeries. You can buy a large quantity and freeze to use when needed and then toast it in a toaster or place it in a hot oven for 5 minutes. Since I do not have a tannour oven, I make this bread in my own kitchen using the regular oven. Sometimes I add black nigella seeds to the dough or sprinkle sesame seeds on top of the dough before it goes into the oven.

Ingredients

3 cups all-purpose flour

1 tablespoon salt

½ teaspoon baking soda

1 tablespoon dry yeast

1 ¼ cups warm water, divided

1 teaspoon sugar

3 tablespoons plain yogurt

3 tablespoons vegetable oil

Preparation

Place the flour, salt, and baking soda in a large bowl and stir. In a small bowl, dissolve the yeast in ¼ cup of the warm water and add the sugar. Set aside for about 10 minutes until the yeast starts to rise, then add to the flour mixture along with the remaining 1 cup warm water. Add the yogurt and knead the mixture to make a soft dough. Oil the bowl and the dough. Cover and let sit for 2 hours in a warm place to rise.

Divide the dough into 6 equal-size balls and arrange on a floured surface. Cover with a cloth and leave to rise for 30 minutes.

Turn the oven broiler to 500 degrees F. Place a baking stone in the oven to preheat for 30 minutes, or you can use a baking sheet.

Roll one of the dough balls on a floured surface. Slap the dough between your palms back and forth a few times to thin out the dough to about 7 inches in diameter. Place it on the floured surface and poke with a fork in multiple places. Brush the surface of the dough with some water. Put the dough on the heated baking stone or baking sheet. Place under the broiler, in the middle rack of the oven, for 3 minutes, until the bread puffs up and becomes lightly browned. Turn the bread over and place under the broiler for 1 minute. Remove from the oven to a rack to cool. Repeat with the rest of the dough balls. Serve hot or warm.

Note: When you bake a large batch of this bread, you can put some baked loaves in freezer bags and store in the freezer for future use. Reheat them in a toaster oven, or take them out of the freezer the night before and leave to thaw on the kitchen counter.

SAMMOUN BREAD

Make 6 pieces

This bread is a fish-shaped loaf and very close to Italian ciabatta bread in flavor. Every neighborhood in Iraq has at least two commercial bakeries to fill the demand for sammoun bread. We typically do not bake this bread at home, but I attempted to bake it in my own kitchen and was very pleased with the flavor and its resemblance to the sammoun bread found in bakeries. You need to use high-gluten bread flour so that the bread comes out chewy like pizza dough. For best result, after the dough rises, put the dough in the refrigerator to chill overnight or as long as six hours before you shape it and bake it.

Ingredients

1 teaspoon dry yeast

1 teaspoon sugar

1¼ cups warm water, divided

1 teaspoon salt

3 cups white bread flour

1 teaspoon oil for the bowl

Preparation

In a bowl, dissolve the yeast and sugar in ¼ cup warm water and set aside for about 10 minutes to activate. Add the salt to the flour. When the yeast begins to rise, add it to the flour along with the remaining 1 cup of warm water and knead the dough for 5 minutes. When the dough is soft but not sticky, place it in an oiled bowl and cover with a kitchen towel. Leave it to rise for 2 hours.

Punch down the dough and divide into 6 balls and arrange on a floured work surface. On a floured board, roll each of the dough balls and shape into flat ovals with pointed ends (the shape of a fish). Place on a floured pan. Slash the tops of the breads with a knife. Cover and leave in a warm place to rise for 1 hour.

Heat the oven to 450 degrees F. Place a baking pan or baking stone on the middle rack in the oven to heat it.

Brush the surface of the breads with a mixture of water and sugar to give them a golden color when baked. Arrange the breads on the preheated pan in the oven. Pour ½ cup of water on the bottom of the oven to create steam. Bake for 10 to 15 minutes until golden brown. Remove from the pan and place on a wire rack to cool. When cool, put the loaves in plastic bags to prevent them from drying and use the same day.

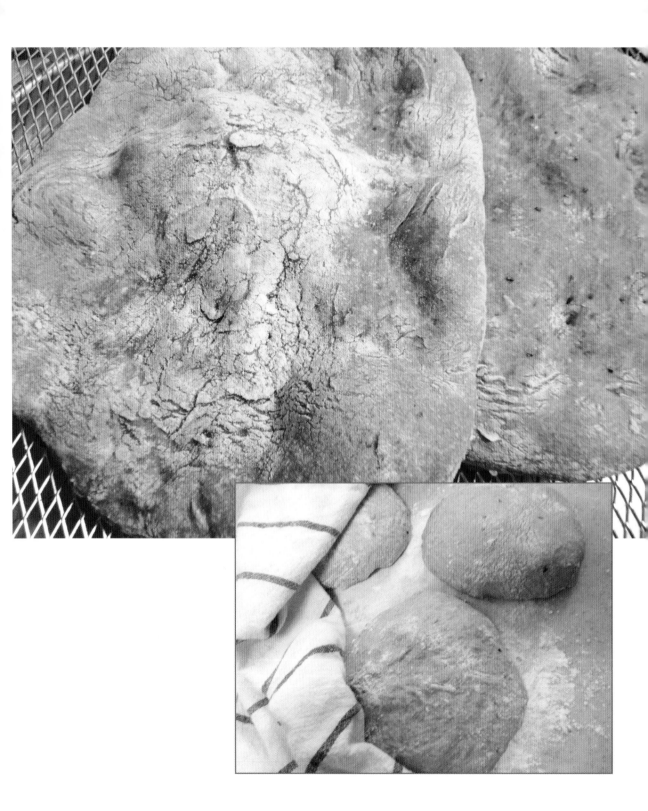

WHOLE WHEAT FLATBREAD

KHUBIZ SHAEER

Makes 3 pieces

This is very healthful bread that my sister makes every week for her family. You will find this bread very satisfying with cheeses, soups, and salads. To make a less dense dough, you can substitute 1 cup of white flour for 1 cup of the whole wheat flour. Whole wheat flour absorbs more water so you need to adjust the water according to your flour. You could also use rye flour for this recipe.

Ingredients

1 tablespoon dry yeast

1 teaspoon sugar

1½ cups warm water, divided

3 cups whole wheat flour

1 teaspoon salt

1 teaspoon nigella seeds

1 teaspoon baking soda

1 teaspoon oil for the bowl

Preparation

In a bowl, put the yeast and sugar in ½ cup of the warm water and stir. Cover the bowl for 10 minutes until the yeast is activated.

Stir together the flour, salt, nigella seeds, and baking soda. Make a well in the middle of the flour and add the yeast mixture and remaining 1 cup of warm water. Knead the dough for 5 minutes. It should be moist and sticky. Put the dough in an oiled bowl, cover with a towel, and leave to rise for 1 hour.

When the dough has risen, punch it down, and divide into 3 balls. Place them on a floured work surface, cover with a towel, and allow to rise again for 1 hour.

Using a rolling pin or a dowel, roll out the dough balls to 9 inches in diameter on a floured work surface. Place the dough disks on a tray to rise for 30 minutes, covered with a towel. Preheat oven to 500 degrees F.

Take a fork and poke some holes into the dough disks. Brush the surfaces with water and place them on a baking tray. Bake for 10 minutes. Remove from oven and place the flatbreads on a wire rack to cool. Serve with lunch or dinner and with stews.

Baklava

DESSERTS

Desserts

There are many types of *baklawa*, western-style cakes, candies, and cookies that are commercially available at special *Halawiyat* stores in Iraq. I tried to include in this section a variety of traditional desserts, like *halawa*, puddings, *baklawa*, *klecha*, and cookies, that we prepared at home for holidays and special occasions.

HALVA HALAWA

Halawa is a dessert that resembles fudge. There are different commercial varieties of *halawa* made with *tahini*, sesame seeds, or carrots. They are flavored with rosewater, cardamom, or cinnamon. My mother used to make these recipes often, and we used to snack on them as candy. When she made these recipes for Lent, she replaced the butter with sesame paste (*tahini*).

HALVA WITH DATE SYRUP

HALAWA BIL DIBIS

6 to 8 servings

If you are unable to find date syrup in Middle Eastern grocery stores, you can make your own (see page 67). You can also use honey or natural maple syrup, but the flavor will not be the same as the date syrup.

Ingredients

½ cup unsalted butter

2 cups all-purpose flour

½ teaspoon salt

1 teaspoon ground cinnamon

1 cup date syrup (*dibis*, page 67)

3 tablespoons sugar

½ cup walnut halves

½ cup whole pistachios

Preparation

Melt the butter in a heavy saucepan and add the flour and salt. Sauté for 8 minutes until the flour turns golden brown. Add the cinnamon and stir. Remove from heat.

In a separate pan, bring ½ cup of water to a boil and add the date syrup and sugar. Stir the mixture until the sugar dissolves. Add this mixture slowly to the flour mixture. Stir vigorously on low heat until the mixture turns smooth and silky.

Pour the mixture onto a plate to a thickness of 1-inch and decorate with walnuts and pistachios.

HALVA WITH MILK

HALAWA BIL HALEEB

6 to 8 servings

For this recipe, you can replace the water used in traditional halva with milk and add rosewater for flavoring.

Ingredients

½ cup unsalted butter

2 cups all-purpose flour

½ teaspoon salt

1 teaspoon ground cardamom

½ cup milk

1 cup sugar

½ cup chopped walnuts

1 cup walnut halves for decoration

⅓ cup toasted pistachios for
   decoration

Preparation

Melt the butter in a heavy saucepan and add the flour and salt. Sauté for 8 minutes until the flour turns a golden color. Add the cardamom and stir. Remove from heat.

In a separate pan, bring the milk to a boil and add the sugar. Stir the mixture until the sugar is dissolved. Add this mixture slowly to the flour mixture and stir vigorously over low heat until smooth and silky. Fold in the chopped walnuts and pour the mixture onto a plate. It should be about 1-inch thick. Decorate with walnut halves and pistachios. Serve at room temperature.

SESAME HALVA

HALAWAT MOSUL

6 to 8 servings

This halawa *is made only in Mosul. Every year during Lent, my sister Samar buys this commercially made* halawa *and sends me some. It is very delicious and we serve it after Arabic coffee. You could use honey or natural maple syrup instead of date syrup.*

Ingredients

½ cup sugar

½ cup date syrup (*dibis*, page 67)

2 tablespoons tahini

1 tablespoon vinegar

1 teaspoon baking soda

1 ½ cups toasted sesame seeds

1 teaspoon ground cardamom

½ cup chopped walnuts

Pistachios and almonds for decoration

Preparation

Oil a 9x13-inch baking pan and set aside. Combine the sugar and date syrup in a saucepan. Bring to a boil, stirring constantly. Reduce the heat without stirring. Add the tahini and stir. Add the vinegar and leave it to simmer for 5 minutes. When the mixture reaches 300 degrees F on a candy thermometer, remove from heat.

Stir in the baking soda and add the sesame seeds, cardamom, and walnuts. Pour into the prepared pan and spread evenly. Decorate with pistachios and almonds. Let cool before you break into pieces or shape into rounds. Store in a tight container or wrap in foil and put in a freezer bag and freeze until ready to use.

CARROT HALVA

HALAWAT JIZAR

6 to 8 servings

This is a very delicious halawa *but it takes a lot of time to prepare. It always reminds me of my travels when I was still living in Iraq. I used to visit the city of Najaf, which is located in Karbala province south of Baghdad, and I made sure to buy the local specialty—carrot* halawa. *Years later, my sister Samar sent me her recipe and I attempted to make it. It tastes very close to the factory-made* halawa, *but the commercial* halawa *is darker in color and more like taffy.*

Ingredients

1 pound carrots, shredded

¼ cup vegetable oil or unsalted
   butter

1 cup sugar

1 tablespoon lemon juice

½ teaspoon ground cardamom

1 teaspoon cornstarch

½ cup chopped walnuts

Preparation

Place the carrots and 1 cup of water in a pot. Bring to a boil and then reduce the heat and simmer for 30 minutes, uncovered, until the carrots are very soft and the water is almost evaporated. Add the oil or butter and leave to simmer for 10 more minutes.

Put the mixture in a food processor and purée it (or use an immersion blender). Pour it back into the pot and add the sugar and lemon juice. Cook over low heat, stirring constantly, for 20 minutes. Add the cardamom and stir.

Dissolve the cornstarch in 1 tablespoon of water and add to the *halawa* and stir. Keep cooking, stirring constantly, until the *halawa* leaves the sides of the pot (then you know that all the moisture is evaporated and the *halawa* is ready to take off the heat). Spread it on a flat dish to about ½-inch thick and decorate with the walnuts.

MANNA FROM HEAVEN

MANNA EL SAMMA

Makes 10 to 12 pieces

I never thought I would be able to make this halawa *in my own kitchen. We always purchased kilos of this flavorful candy from the factory. My father used to buy 20 pounds of it and bring it home where we all gathered in the kitchen around the table to assemble the* manna halawa. *We also called this* halawa *"Halawat Khither Elias" to celebrate the memory of Saint Khither Elias.*

We took a small piece of the candy the size of a walnut and filled the center of it with walnuts or pistachios. Then we rolled the clusters in flour and arranged them on a floured tray. The flour helped prevent the clusters from sticking together. The candy was kept in tight containers or in the refrigerator. We served these with Arabic coffee.

I tried to make this halawa *a few times, but it did not come out right. My sister Samar emailed me her recipe, which I then adapted a little to make the* halawa *firm and easy to work with. I found out using less honey did the trick. In this recipe, I do not fill the* halawa *with walnuts, but stir the walnuts into it to make clusters.*

Ingredients

½ cup honey

1 cup sugar

3 egg whites

1 teaspoon ground cardamom

1 cup walnuts

½ cup unsalted almonds or
  pistachios

2 cups flour for rolling

Preparation

Pour the honey and sugar into a nonstick pot and stir. Whip the egg whites for a few minutes until stiff. Fold them into the honey and sugar. Place the pot over low heat and stir constantly for 40 minutes, until the mixture begins to thicken and leaves the sides of the pot. Sprinkle cardamom over the mixture and stir. Add the walnuts and almonds and mix thoroughly.

Spread the flour on a tray. Using a tablespoon, drop clusters of the honey mixture on the floured tray. Then roll the clusters in flour so that they do not stick together. Arrange them in a container and cover them with more flour. Store at room temperature or keep in the refrigerator.

SESAME CANDY

SIMSIMIYA

Makes 12 pieces

This is a very popular candy that is sold by street vendors and candy shops. You can prepare a thick syrup and pour it over the toasted sesame seeds but this recipe is more healthful as I use natural honey and raw sugar.

Ingredients

2 cups sesame seeds

½ cup honey

½ cup raw sugar

½ teaspoon ground cinnamon or
   ground cardamom

Preparation

Pour the sesame seeds into a pan and stir over medium heat for 5 minutes, until lightly toasted. Set aside.

Pour the honey in a pan and bring to a boil. Add the sugar and swirl, but do not stir. When the mixture turns light brown, remove from heat. Add the cinnamon and stir. Pour the honey mixture over the sesame seeds and stir until all seeds are well coated.

Pour the mixture into a well-oiled 9x13-inch pan. Place foil over the candy and smooth the surface. Remove the foil and smooth the surface again with a lightly oiled hand. Either cut the candy into squares while still warm or, as I prefer, take small pieces of the candy and roll it in your hands to make sesame balls.

DATE SESAME BALLS

KURAT IL TAMIR

Makes 15 balls

You can find pitted pressed baking dates in Middle Eastern grocery stores, or you could put pitted majdool dates in a food processor and pulse them a few times to make a paste.

Ingredients

1 pound pitted baking dates

1 cup toasted sesame seeds, divided

1 tablespoon tahini

1 cup walnuts, chopped

1 teaspoon ground cardamom or
   cinnamon

½ cup shredded coconut

Preparation

Put the dates, ½ cup sesame seeds, and tahini in a food processor. Pulse a few times and then add the walnuts and spice. Pulse again until coarsely chopped.

Take the mixture out and make small balls. Roll half of the balls in the remaining ½ cup sesame seeds, and the other half in the shredded coconut. Serve with coffee.

PUDDINGS

Iraqi puddings are made with either rice or cornstarch in combination with milk and sugar. They are usually decorated with nuts or ground cinnamon and served after heavy meals. Puddings tend to form a skin on the surface as they cool, so after pouring the pudding in serving bowls, sprinkle sugar on top to keep the surface moist, and cover the bowl tightly with plastic wrap before you refrigerate.

When I was growing up in Iraq, we purchased canned English custard powder called Bird's Custard to make pudding. We added this yellow-colored powder to milk and sugar and cooked it on top of the stove until it thickened. It had vanilla flavor and was easy to prepare. You can find it in international markets or online.

CORNSTARCH PUDDING

MAHALLABI

This is a delicious, light, easy-to-make dessert. We serve it after heavy meals or as a snack during the day.

Ingredients

2 cups milk, divided

4 tablespoons sugar

5 tablespoons cornstarch

1 teaspoon rosewater or ½ teaspoon ground cardamom or ground cinnamon

Pistachios for decoration

Preparation

In a small pot, bring 1½ cups of milk to a boil. Reduce heat. Add the sugar and stir. Mix the cornstarch in the remaining ½ cup of milk and pour into the pot. Keep stirring until the pudding thickens. (Make sure it does not burn when it sticks to the bottom of the pot.)

Remove from heat and stir in the rosewater or spice. Pour pudding into small custard cups and decorate with pistachios. Refrigerate for a few hours before serving.

RICE PUDDING

RIZ BIL HALEEB

4 servings

This dessert, in its many variations, is very popular throughout the world. The Iraqi recipe is simple, but you can embellish it with nuts and raisins.

Ingredients

1 cup basmati rice

3 cups milk

½ cup sugar

½ teaspoon salt

1 cinnamon stick

½ teaspoon ground cardamom

1 teaspoon rosewater

Nuts or ground cinnamon for
    decoration

Preparation

Soak the rice in a bowl of water for 30 minutes. Drain and set aside.

Pour the milk in a pot and add the sugar, salt, and cinnamon stick. Stir the mixture and add the rice. Cook for 45 minutes, uncovered, on low heat. Make sure to watch the pot and stir the pudding occasionally so the rice doesn't stick to the pot.

When the rice is cooked and the mixture becomes thick, remove it from heat, remove cinnamon stick, and add the cardamom and rosewater. Stir and pour into a deep dish or small custard dishes. Decorate with nuts or ground cinnamon. Cover with plastic wrap and chill before serving.

RICE PUDDING WITH SAFFRON

ZERDE

4 servings

This is a very popular dessert throughout the Middle East. It is served at weddings and birth celebrations. It is also prepared specifically during the first ten days of the Islamic holy month of Muharram which commemorates the death of Imam Al Hussein. We had Shia neighbors who distributed plates of this dessert throughout the neighborhood at that time of year. It was a very welcome treat.

Ingredients

1 cup basmati rice

1 cinnamon stick

½ cup sugar

½ teaspoon saffron

1 tablespoon rosewater

Ground cinnamon

Preparation

Wash rice and soak in water for 30 minutes. Drain and rub the rice in your hands to break the rice grains. Alternatively, you could pulse it 4 times in a food processor.

In a large pot, bring 4 cups of water to a boil. Add rice and cinnamon stick and cook, uncovered, on medium heat for 20 minutes.

When rice is cooked, stir in sugar and saffron. Reduce heat to simmer and keep stirring until the consistency of the pudding resembles oatmeal. Remove from heat. Remove cinnamon stick and stir in rosewater.

Transfer the pudding to a plate or small serving bowls. Sprinkle ground cinnamon on top or garnish with nuts. Chill the pudding for at least 4 hours before serving.

CAKES

Iraqis enjoy desserts. There are many varieties of commercially made cakes available that are decorated with icing and sold in special *halawiyat* stores. Street vendors also carry trays stacked with pieces of plain yellow cake. We learned how to make European desserts at home using chocolate, imported cocoa powder, and powdered sugar. To ensure authenticity here I have chosen to list only the cakes and ingredients I grew up enjoying.

ORANGE CAKE

CAKE BIL BURTUGAL

My mother always had a piece of cake with her breakfast, and she kept cakes in the freezer too. In the winter, since oranges are a winter fruit, she dried orange peel, ground it, and kept it in a jar to use as flavoring for this cake.

Ingredients

1 cup unsalted butter, at room temperature

1½ cups sugar

3 eggs

2½ cups cake flour (more or less, depending on the flour), divided

½ cup fresh orange juice (the juice of about 2 oranges)

½ cup warm water

½ cup finely chopped orange peel

½ teaspoon ground cardamom

1½ teaspoons baking powder

½ teaspoon salt

Preparation

Butter and flour a tube cake pan. Preheat oven to 350 degrees F.

Place the butter in a bowl, add the sugar and beat for 5 minutes, until it becomes creamy. In another bowl, beat the eggs until they become light in color. Slowly add the eggs and 1 cup of flour to the butter mixture and mix. Add orange juice and 1 more cup of flour and mix. Add warm water and orange peel. Then add cardamom, baking powder, salt, and the remaining ½ cup of flour. Stir well.

Pour the batter into prepared tube cake pan. Bake 45 minutes, or until a knife inserted comes out clean. Leave the cake in the pan for 25 minutes to cool completely before you turn it out onto a wire rack. Serve when cool.

RAISIN WALNUT CAKE

CAKE BIL JOZ WIL KISHMISH

10 to 12 servings

This is a special spice cake that my mother used to make during the Christmas and New Year holidays. You can keep this cake in the freezer for a few months. Wrap it in foil and put it in a freezer bag. Take it out of the freezer the night before you plan to serve it.

Ingredients

1 cup unsalted butter, at room temperature

1½ cups sugar, plus 1 tablespoon for topping

3 eggs

2½ cups cake flour (more or less, depending on the flour)

1 teaspoon salt

1 cup warm water

1 teaspoon ground cardamom

½ teaspoon ground cinnamon

Pinch ground nutmeg

1½ teaspoons baking powder

½ cup golden raisins

1½ cup chopped walnuts

Preparation

Butter and flour a tube cake pan. Preheat oven to 350 degrees F.

Place the butter and sugar in a bowl and beat for 5 minutes, until it becomes creamy. In another bowl, beat the eggs until they become light in color. While beating the butter, slowly add the eggs, half of the flour, and the salt. Beat well. Add ½ cup of the warm water and mix. Add spices, remaining flour, and baking powder. Beat and add the remaining ½ cup of warm water. Add the raisins and 1 cup of the walnuts and stir with a spatula.

Pour batter into the prepared tube pan and sprinkle the top with the remaining ½ cup of chopped walnuts and 1 tablespoon of sugar. Bake on middle rack for 50 minutes or until a knife inserted comes out clean. Keep in pan for 25 minutes to cool before you turn the cake out on a wire rack.

DATE NUT BREAD

CAKE BIL TAMIR

8 to 10 servings

This is one of my favorite light breads that I bake very often. Dried dates are my favored fruit for after dinner or daytime snacking. The combination of dates and cardamom is delicious. This bread tastes even better the next day.

Ingredients

1 cup chopped dates (about 20 pitted dates)

1 egg

⅔ cup sugar

¼ cup vegetable oil

2 tablespoons melted unsalted butter

2 cups cake flour

½ teaspoon salt

1 teaspoon ground cardamom

½ teaspoon ground cinnamon

1 tablespoon baking powder

1¼ cup chopped walnuts

Preparation

Oil a 9x5-inch loaf pan and dust it with flour (or oil a piece of parchment paper and line the bread pan with it). Preheat oven to 350 degrees F.

Put the dates in a bowl and pour in 1 cup of boiling water. Leave them to soak for 15 minutes to soften.

In a separate bowl, beat the egg and add half of the sugar. Add half of the water-and-date mixture and mix with a wooden spoon. Add the oil, butter, the rest of the sugar, and 1 cup of flour and mix. Add the rest of the flour and the remaining water-and-date mixture, and stir well to make sure all the flour is well blended. Add the salt, cardamom, cinnamon, baking powder, and 1 cup of the walnuts and stir.

Pour the batter in the prepared pan and sprinkle remaining ¼ cup chopped walnuts on top. Place the pan on middle rack in the oven and bake for 1 hour. Leave bread to cool in pan for 15 minutes. Turn the bread out on a wire rack to cool completely. Once cool you can wrap it in foil and refrigerate it or freeze it for later use.

It is believed that around the 8th century BC, the Assyrians were the first people to put chopped nuts and dried fruit together between a few layers of thin bread dough and then add honey and bake it in their wood burning ovens. This earliest known version of baklava was baked only on special occasions and served to the kings and the wealthy.

BAKLAVA

BAKLAWA

Baklava is the most popular dessert in Iraq and the Middle East. This delicious combination of phyllo dough filled with nuts, sugar, and butter comes in many shapes and sizes. It is stacked, coiled, made into sticks, and folded. Once you practice and learn how to handle the phyllo dough, you can use it in many creative dishes.

When I make baklawa, I always remember my Aunt Matheela (who was the baker in the house), and how she used to spend a whole day making the dough and rolling it out on a large circular table using a dowel. Each sheet of dough was layered on a large circular tray 25 inches in diameter. Then she spread a layer of crushed walnuts mixed with crushed sugarcane and ground cardamom. She added a few more layers of dough and spread another layer of the walnut mixture. She topped it with a few more layers of dough and then poured clarified butter on top and cut the baklawa into large diamonds, 4 inches long by 3 inches wide and 2 inches high. Each piece used to feed 3 people! The tray was then carried on the head to a public neighborhood bakery to bake. As soon as it came out of the oven, they poured cold syrup over it.

My mother used to make baklawa too, with the help of my Aunt Najma and grandmother Jameela who lived with us in Baghdad. She followed the same recipe, but she cut it in 2-inch-long by 1-inch high pieces and it was much lighter than my aunt's recipe. The whole family participated in the very involved process. As children, we used to crack the walnuts for the filling, and we enjoyed being in the kitchen. If you are an experienced pastry chef you can make the phyllo dough (see page 273), otherwise buy the pre-made frozen packages as they work very well.

When I came to the United States, I began making a lighter version of baklawa which I have provided here.

Ingredients

1 pound shelled walnuts

⅔ cup sugar

1 teaspoon ground cardamom or
   ground cinnamon

¾ pound unsalted butter

1 pound frozen phyllo dough, thawed

1 cup homemade sugar syrup (page
   272) or honey

(Recipe continues on next page.)

BAKLAVA (CONTINUED)

Preparation

Preheat oven to 350 degrees F. Butter a 17¾x12x1-inch jelly roll pan.

Chop the walnuts and mix them with the sugar and cardamom or cinnamon and set aside.

To clarify the butter, put butter in a small pot or saucepan. Melt on top of the stove over low heat making sure not to burn the butter. Skim off the foam that develops on top with a spoon. Remove from heat and let it rest for a few minutes. (You could also melt the butter in the microwave.) Spoon the clear butter into a glass container. Discard the milk solids in the bottom.

Open the package of phyllo dough and place the layers on the work surface and cover with a kitchen towel. Layer 8 sheets of phyllo on the prepared pan, brushing each layer gently with some of the clarified butter. Sprinkle on the walnut mixture. Top the walnuts with 12 more layers of phyllo, making sure to butter each layer.

Cut the pastry into diamond shapes and bake for 25 to 30 minutes, until golden brown. Drizzle the syrup or honey over it as soon as it comes out of the oven. Cut again and keep in a tightly closed container. You can refrigerate or freeze it to store.

SUGAR SYRUP FOR DESSERTS

2 cups water

2 cups sugar

1 cinnamon stick

1 tablespoon lemon juice

1 tablespoon rosewater (optional)

In a pot, bring water and sugar to a boil and stir. Add the cinnamon stick and swirl. Simmer for 20 minutes. Add the lemon juice and simmer for 10 more minutes. Remove from heat and add the rosewater if you prefer. Remove and discard cinnamon stick. Cool syrup before pouring it over the dessert. Use syrup on Baklava, Phyllo Stuffed with Pudding (page 274), Phyllo Sticks (page 275), and Bird Nests (page 277).

PHYLLO DOUGH

AJEENAT IL BAKLAWA

The method for making phyllo has not changed since ancient times. Middle Eastern cooks prefer to stretch the dough with their hands. It takes a great deal of practice and skill and is very time consuming. Families who live in the countryside make sure to train their young girls in this process. When these girls are married, they will pass the skill to their children.

Fortunately, if you don't have the time or patience to make your own dough, frozen ready-made phyllo is available for purchase at grocery stores now. You simply need to thaw it before using.

Note: For this recipe you need to use a dowel that is 36 inches long and ¾ inch in diameter. You can have it cut at a hardware store.

Ingredients

4 cups all-purpose flour

2 egg yolks

1½ cups water, plus more if needed

1 pound cornstarch

Preparation

Put flour in a bowl and make a well in the middle. Beat egg yolks and add 1½ cups water. Pour the mixture slowly into the well of the flour and combine well. Add a few more tablespoons of water if needed to make a pliable dough. Knead the dough for 5 minutes, until it becomes smooth. Cover with a kitchen towel and leave to rest for 30 minutes.

Divide the dough into 12 small balls and keep them covered with a towel to prevent them from drying. Dust your work surface with cornstarch and start rolling out one of the dough balls with the dowel to make a big circle, dusting it frequently with cornstarch. Continue to roll out, shifting the dowel on the dough until the dough is very thin and is about 25 inches in diameter.

Roll the dough around the dowel and unroll the dough on a large circular tray. Cover with clean sheets to prevent it from drying. Continue the process with the rest of the dough, and stack each sheet on top of the other, sprinkling cornstarch between them, until all balls are rolled out. Use the dough immediately for any of the recipes calling for phyllo.

PHYLLO STUFFED WITH PUDDING

FATAYER-ZINOOD IL SIT

6 servings

These are phyllo rolls filled with custard and baked in the oven. For the filling, you use the recipe for Cornstarch Pudding but add 7 tablespoons of cornstarch instead of 5 to make the pudding thicker and easier to spoon over the phyllo. The syrup must be prepared ahead of time and cooled before you pour it over the rolls when they come out of the oven. I prefer to use honey.

Ingredients

6 frozen phyllo sheets (from a 1
  pound package), thawed

1 cup unsalted butter, melted

Cornstarch Pudding (page 263, made
  with 7 tablespoons cornstarch),
  cooled

1 cup homemade sugar syrup (page
  272) or honey

Berry jam or pistachios for decoration

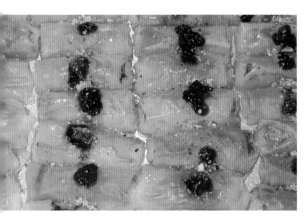

Preparation

Preheat oven to 350 degrees F. Place 1 phyllo sheet on a cutting board. Brush it gently with some of the melted butter. Fold it in half. Pipe 1 tablespoon of pudding along one side of the phyllo. Fold the phyllo over the pudding and fold the sides towards the center. Roll it to the end of the sheet (as for an egg roll). Place it on a baking sheet with the seam down. (You can also fold it into a triangle just like folding the flag or into squares.) Repeat with the other sheets of phyllo.

Brush the tops of the rolls with butter. Bake for 20 minutes, until golden brown.

Pour cold syrup or honey over the rolls as soon as they come out of the oven. Serve warm the same day. Decorate the tops with berry jam or chopped pistachios.

PHYLLO STICKS

BURMA

My sister Samar makes this recipe very often. It is light and does not need a lot of filling.

Ingredients

¾ pound walnuts or pistachios, chopped

½ cup sugar

1 teaspoon ground cardamom or ground cinnamon

1 pound frozen phyllo dough, thawed

½ pound unsalted butter, melted

a dowel or handle of a wooden spoon

1 cup honey or homemade sugar syrup (page 272)

Preparation

Preheat oven to 350 degrees F. Oil a baking sheet.

Combine the walnuts or pistachios, sugar, and cardamom or cinnamon in a bowl. Stir and set aside.

Place 1 sheet of phyllo on a cutting board. Brush with some of the melted butter. Place the dowel across the short end of the buttered phyllo sheet. Sprinkle 1 tablespoon of the nut filling along the dowel. Fold the edge closest to you over the dowel and roll it to the end of the sheet. Squeeze the ends of the phyllo roll and push towards the center to form pleats like an accordion. Slide out the dowel and place the phyllo roll seam down on prepared baking sheet. Brush with butter. Continue with the rest of the phyllo.

Bake for 20 to 25 minutes until golden in color. Take out of the oven and immediately pour honey or sugar syrup over the rolls.

BIRD NESTS

ISH IL ASFOOR

You can prepare the filling the day before. Place the package of frozen phyllo in the refrigerator to thaw overnight. If you do not have a dowel, use the handle of a wooden spoon. The name "bird nests" is appropriate because the phyllo is shaped into a coil and you fill the center with pistachios or walnuts.

Ingredients

¾ pound walnuts or pistachios,
   chopped
½ cup sugar
1 teaspoon ground cardamom or
   ground cinnamon
1 pound frozen phyllo dough, thawed
½ pound unsalted butter, melted
a dowel or handle of a wooden spoon
1 cup honey or homemade sugar
   syrup (page 272)

Preparation

Preheat oven to 375 degrees F. Oil a muffin pan.

Combine the walnuts or pistachios, sugar, and cardamom or cinnamon in a bowl. Stir and set aside.

Remove the phyllo dough from the box and place it on a cutting board. Cover with a dish towel to prevent it from drying.

Place 1 pastry sheet on a cutting board and brush with some of the melted butter. Place another layer of phyllo on top and brush it with some butter. Fold the phyllo in half to make a rectangle.

Place a dowel along the side of the phyllo and fold the phyllo over it. Roll the dowel to the other side of the phyllo sheet. Squeeze both ends of the phyllo roll and push towards the center to form pleats like an accordion. Slide the dowel out. Bring the edges of the phyllo roll together to make a circle. Repeat with remaining phyllo sheets.

Place each of the pastries in a muffin cup. Brush with more melted butter. Sprinkle the nut filling in the middle of the circles. Bake for 15 to 20 minutes. Remove from the oven and immediately pour the honey or syrup over them. When cool, place in a plastic container and refrigerate if you are not going to serve the same day.

ALMOND COOKIES

LOUZINA

Makes 18

We usually use blanched raw almonds for this recipe. If you blanch them yourself be sure to dry them before grinding.

Ingredients

2 cups blanched almonds

¾ cup sugar

1 teaspoon baking powder

¼ cup all-purpose flour

½ teaspoon ground cardamom

2 egg whites (¼ cup)

1 teaspoon rosewater

Whole blanched almonds for
    decoration

Preparation

Preheat oven to 350 degrees F. Line a baking sheet with parchment paper or silicone sheet.

Put the almonds and sugar in a food processor and pulse until all almonds are ground. Add the baking powder, flour, and cardamom and combine.

Whip the egg whites for 3 minutes, until foaming, and gradually fold into the almond mixture with the rosewater. Take small pieces of dough the size of a walnut and shape them into triangles, stars, or circles.

Arrange cookies on the prepared baking sheet. Place a blanched whole almond on top of each cookie. Bake for 25 minutes. Store in a tightly closed container.

CARDAMOM COOKIES

SHAKAR LAMA

Makes 15 to 20

These are the Iraqi version of butter cookies. We bake these cookies and keep them in a cookie container or freeze them for when we have unexpected guests—which happens very often. We take them out of the freezer and they thaw within 1 hour.

Ingredients

1 cup unsalted butter, room temperature

1½ cups sugar

2¼ cups all-purpose flour

½ teaspoon salt

1 teaspoon ground cardamom

½ teaspoon baking powder

Blanched almonds for decoration

Preparation

Preheat oven to 350 degrees F. Line a baking sheet with parchment paper.

In a bowl, cream the butter and sugar until fluffy and set aside.

In another bowl combine the flour, salt, cardamom, and baking powder.

Add the flour mixture to the butter mixture. Mix well using your hands. Take walnut-size pieces of the dough and roll them into balls and then press flat. Arrange the cookies on prepared pan. Decorate the top of the cookies with almonds. Bake for 25 minutes. Leave them on the pan to cool for 15 minutes. Store in a tightly closed container.

COCONUT MACAROONS

JOZ IL HIND

If you have to use the sweetened coconut you find at most grocery stores, use only half a cup of sugar. I prefer to use unsweetened shredded coconut that can be found at Asian and Middle Eastern grocery stores.

Ingredients

- 3 cups shredded unsweetened coconut
- 2 tablespoons flour or cornstarch
- 1 teaspoon baking powder
- 1 teaspoon ground cardamom
- 3 egg whites (½ cup)
- 1 cup granulated sugar
- 2 tablespoons rosewater

Preparation

Preheat oven to 350 degrees F. Line a baking sheet with parchment paper or a silicone sheet.

Put the coconut in a bowl. Combine with the flour, baking powder, and cardamom. Set aside.

In a bowl, whisk the egg whites until foaming and then add sugar. Beat for 2 minutes. Pour over the coconut mixture and mix together by hand. Add the rosewater and mix in by hand. Set aside for 5 minutes.

Shape the dough into walnut-size balls. Arrange the macaroons on the parchment paper. Bake for 20 minutes. Remove the pan from the oven and leave cookies to cool for 10 minutes.

HOLIDAY COOKIES
KLECHA

When I was very young, my mother, grandmother, and aunts used to gather in the kitchen to prepare klecha for Christmas or Easter. They made two extra-large trays of cookies and then our housekeeper carried the trays on her head to the bakery to bake them in the big bread oven. Later in the 1950s, we bought a gas stove with a large oven which accommodated large, rectangular cookie sheets. Although these cookies are baked for the holidays and big feasts, we make sure to keep a few bags in the freezer to serve our guests throughout the year. Klechas are made with a choice of walnut filling or date filling—both are delicious.

Ingredients

Dough:

2 packets dry yeast

1 ½ cups warm water

6 cups all-purpose flour

1 teaspoon nigella seeds

1 teaspoon ground cardamom

1 tablespoon salt

1 teaspoon ground fennel seeds

¾ pound (3 sticks) unsalted butter

Oil for bowl

1 egg, beaten for egg wash

Walnut filling:

1 cup walnuts, chopped

3 tablespoons sugar

½ teaspoon ground cardamom

Preparation

Dough:
In a small bowl, put the yeast in ½ cup of the warm water and cover to rise for about 10 minutes. Combine the flour, nigella seeds, cardamom, salt, and ground fennel seeds. Rub the butter into the flour mixture with your hands. Add yeast mixture and remaining 1 cup of warm water. Knead the dough, adding more water if needed, to make a smooth dough. Place in a large oiled bowl, cover, and let rise in a warm place for 1 hour.

While the dough is rising, prepare the fillings:

Walnut filling:
In a bowl, mix chopped walnuts, sugar, and cardamom. Set aside.

(Ingredients and Preparation continued on next page)

HOLIDAY COOKIES (CONTINUED)

Date filling:

8 ounces soft baking dates or
   majdool dates

2 tablespoons unsalted butter

½ teaspoon ground cardamom

½ teaspoon ground cinnamon

Date Filling:
In a pan, sauté dates in butter until soft and easy to spread. Add ground cardamom and cinnamon. Let the mixture cool. Cover a cutting board with plastic wrap and spread the dates on the board using a rolling pin to make a thin sheet.

Assembly
Preheat oven to 350 degrees F. Oil baking sheets and set aside.

Take half of the dough and roll it out on a floured work surface with a rolling pin to ¼-inch thick. Cut circles using a cookie cutter or a glass. Put 1 teaspoon of the filling in the middle of each circle. Fold circles in half-moon shape. Crimp the edges. Arrange on the oiled baking sheet. Brush with egg wash and bake for 30 to 35 minutes. Remove from pan and cool on a rack.

Roll out the other half of the dough on a cutting board to ½ inch thick. Cover the top with a very thin layer of date mixture. Roll the dough like a jelly roll. Cut into 1-inch-wide slices and arrange slices on the oiled baking sheet with the dough facing up and cut side on sides. Brush tops of cookies with egg wash and bake for 30 minutes. Put the cookies on cooling rack. Store in a cookie container.

Serve cookies with tea.

THE DATE PALM: IRAQ'S NATIONAL TREE

The date palm tree has been considered a symbol of fertility since ancient times, and it is the most important fruit tree in Iraq. Date export was a major industry in Iraq until the recent wars and diseases that diminished the date industry. Iraq was once home to 13 million palm trees and exported 130,000 tons of dates to the rest of the world.

Date palm trees grow in the middle and southern parts of Iraq. Nomads planted these date palm trees at oases in the deserts, thus supplementing the Bedouin diet of milk products and bread.

The palm tree is pollinated once a year in April. The fruit is borne in large clusters at the top of the trunk. In August, the dangling fruit clusters are green and then they turn yellow and light brown when ripe. In September or October the dates are harvested. Each tree yields about 200 pounds of dates. The dates can be eaten fresh or dried, cooked to make date syrup (*dibis*, page 67), or fermented to make wine and vinegar.

BIBLIOGRAPHY

Books:

Bertman, Stephen. *Handbook of Life in Ancient Mesopotamia*. Facts on File: New York, NY, 2003.

Bottero, Jean. *The Oldest Cuisine in the World*. University of Chicago Press, 2004.

Bottero, Jean. *Everyday Life in Ancient Mesopotamia*. Maryland, Johns Hopkins University Press, 2001.

Cox, Jeff. *The Cook's Herb Garden*. New York, DK Publishing, 2010.

Dalby, Andrew. *Food in the Ancient World From A-Z*. London, Routledge, 2003.

Flandrin, Jean-Louis & Massimo Montanari. *Food: A Culinary History*. Columbia University Press, New York, 1999.

Gilles, Munier. *Iraq: An Illustrated History and Guide*. Massachusetts, Interlink Publishing Group, 2004.

Gordon, Edmund. *Sumerian Proverbs: Glimpses of Everyday Life in Ancient Mesopotamia*. Greenwood Press, N.Y., 1968.

Kaufman, Kathy K. *Cooking in Ancient Civilizations*. Connecticut, Greenwood Press, 2006.

Kazzaz, David. *Mother of the Pound: Memoirs on the Life and History of the Iraqi Jews*. Sepher- Hermon Press, INC., 2001.

Luttinger, Nina. *The Coffee Book*. New York, The New Press, 2006.

"Mesopotamia Yesterday, Iraq Today." Ministry of Information, Iraq, 1977.

Oates, Joan. *Babylon*. Thames and Hudson, London, 1979.

Rhea, Karen. *Daily Life in Ancient Mesopotamia*. Connecticut, Greenwood Press, 1998.

Sabar, Ariel. *My Father's Paradise: A Son's Search for His Jewish Past in Kurdish Iraq*. N.C Bertman, Algonquin Books, 2008.

Steele, Phillip. *Mesopotamia*. New York, DK Publishing, 2007.

Wagner, Heather Lehr. *Iraq*. Philadelphia, Chelsea House Publishing, 2003.

Web, Lois Sinaiko. *Multicultural Cookbook of Life-Cycle Celebrations*. Arizona, Oryx Press, 2000.

Websites:

www.recipesbyrachel.com (for authentic Jewish Iraqi recipes)

www.jewishbook.us/iraqi-jews.html (for Iraqi Jewish customs)

www.nutsonline.com (for Syrian Spice or Arabian Spice)

www.saudiaramcoworld.com (History & Culture)

www.iraqifamilycookbook.com (authentic recipes)

www.bbc.co.uk/history/recent/iraq/

http://www.fao.org/about/en/ (Food and Agricultural Organization)

http://www.library.yale.edu/neareast/exhibitions/cuisine.html (for cuneiform tablets)

RECIPE INDEX

ABOUT THE AUTHOR

Kay Karim was born in Mosul, Iraq, and grew up in Baghdad. She immigrated to the United States with her family in 1968. Kay's knowledge and experience of Iraqi cuisine has been passed down through generations. She and her sisters inherited a treasured collection of family recipes as well as their passion for cooking from their mother and grandmother.

Kay self-published her first cookbook, *Iraqi Family Cookbook: From Mosul to America*, in 2006 to preserve her family's heritage and recipes. The book received the "Special Award of the Jury" of the prestigious Gourmand World Cookbook Awards in 2007. Kay has now expanded the cookbook by adding new regional Iraqi recipes, photos, anecdotes, cooking tips, and notes on Iraqi history and culture.

Kay holds a Masters degree in Library and Information Science from San Jose State University as well as a Masters degree in teaching ESL from Old Dominion University. She works as a librarian, and teaches cooking classes in the Washington, D.C. area, where she has also appeared on local television to give Iraqi cooking demonstrations. She currently resides in Falls Church, Virginia and can be found at www.iraqifamilycookbook.com.

The author with her mother and sisters in Baghdad, 2002. From left to right: her sister May, her mother, Kay, and her sister Samar.

Also available from Hippocrene Books . . .

Afghan Food & Cookery
Helen Saberi

"Helen Saberi writes simply, and with freshness and enthusiasm, of the way of life and of the dishes. Her knowledge and love of the people and the food shine through every page."   —Claudia Roden

Afghanistan has survived centuries of invasion, whether military, cultural or culinary. Its hearty cuisine includes a tempting variety of offerings, of which lamb, pasta, chickpeas, rice pilaf, flat breads, kebabs, spinach, okra, lentils, yogurt, pastries and delicious teas, all flavored with delicate spices, are staple ingredients.

ISBN 978-0-7818-0807-1 · $14.95pb

The Lebanese Cookbook
Hussien Dekmak

"Some of the finest Lebanese food I have ever tasted."
          —Patricia Wells, *International Herald Tribune*

In Lebanon the table is always full. Soups, salads, bread, *mezze*, and entrees are all served at the same time and shared around. The recipes in this book are traditional, home-style cooking prepared with easy-to-get ingredients. You can entertain all tastes by serving a selection of dishes from the various chapters in this wonderful cookbook.

ISBN 978-0-7818-1208-5 · $29.95hc

The Middle Eastern Kitchen
Ghillie Basan

"An insightful and detailed peek into the kitchens of Iran, Turkey, Syria, Lebanon, Jordan, Egypt, Saudi Arabia, and more. The photos by Jonathan Basan are beautiful, whether of goatherds in Yemen, a Lebanese landscape or of dishes such as makloub *(Palestinian rice with chestnuts) or* meghlie *(rice pudding with aniseed) ... a fine book to peruse and to cook from when you feel like being transported to a foreign land, but don't have the time or money to leave home."*

— *New York Daily News*

This remarkable and beautifully illustrated book describes more than 75 ingredients used in Middle Eastern cooking. The insightful texts take readers and cooks into the history and diversity of these ancient cultures, while 150 recipes and color photographs allow them to put their knowledge of these ingredients to practical use.

ISBN 0-7818-1023-X · $29.50hc
ISBN 978-0-7818-1190-3 · $19.50pb

Mama Nazima's Jewish-Iraqi Cuisine
Rivka Goldman

With Mongolian, Turkish and Indian influences, Jewish-Iraqi cuisine is a special blend—and has never been before documented. Rivka Goldman takes the reader through her memories of an ancient land and culture by means of the culinary heritage passed on to her by her mother.

This insightful cookbook memoir describes the many ways in which the unique sociopolitical history of the Jewish-Iraqi has impacted their foods and the ways in which they are eaten, supplying over 100 healthful family recipes. Hearty stuffed vegetables, meat dishes, refreshing salads and much more accompany tales of friendship loyalty, persecution, escape, exile, and of course, celebration.

ISBN 0-7818-1144-9 · $24.95hc

Nile Style: Egyptian Cuisine and Culture
Amy Riolo

"Home cooks of all stripes are sure to savor Riolo's fresh yet authentic approach to Middle Eastern food." —Tim Cebula, *Cooking Light*

"In this eminently useful book, author Amy Riolo satisfies the historical and cultural appetites of cooks by offering updated recipes presented in a classic menu format."
  —Dolores Kostelni, *The Roanoke Times*

This distinctive cookbook features foods that have been prepared since ancient times, long-standing family favorites, modern meals, and original recipes that the author was inspired to create in Egypt. *Nile Style* is the first cookbook devoted to the multi-ethnic and multi-religious history of the Egyptian table.

ISBN 978-0-7818-1221-4 · $29.95hc

Sephardic Israeli Cuisine: A Mediterranean Mosaic
Sheilah Kaufman

Sephardic, derived from the Hebrew word for Spain, defines the Jews of Spain, Portugal, North Africa and the Middle East. The foods of these Mediterranean countries profoundly influenced the Sephardic Israeli cuisine, which abounds with ingredients such as cinnamon, saffron, orange flower water, *tahini* paste, artichokes, fava beans, couscous, bulgur, persimmons, peaches, and limes.

Sephardic Israeli Cuisine offers 120 kosher recipes that celebrate the colorful and delicious culinary mosaic it represents. Using typical Sephardic ingredients, it includes favorites like Yogurt Cheese; Crescent Olive Puffs; Harira: Tamar's Yemenite Chicken Soup; Grilled Fish with Chermoula; Moroccan Cholent; and Moroccan Sweet Potato Pie.

ISBN 0-7818-0926-6 · $24.95hc

Taste of Turkish Cuisine

Nur Ilkin and Sheilah Kaufman

The traditional dishes featured in *A Taste of Turkish Cuisine* make use of a variety of beans, grains, fresh fruits, vegetables, herbs, and, of course, yogurt, one of Turkey's most important contributions to international cuisine. Simple yet rich in flavors, Turkish cuisine resounds of its varied influences, which range from Chinese and Mongolian to Persian and Greek. A history of Turkey's culinary traditions accompanies the 187 recipes, as well as glossaries of commonly used ingredients and Turkish cooking terms.

ISBN 0-7818-0948-7· $24.95hc

A Pied Noir Cookbook: French Sephardic Cuisine from Algeria

Chantal Clabrough

This unique cookbook relates the story of the Pied Noir or "Black Feet," Sephardic Jews from the North African nation of Algeria. The cuisine of the Pied Noir reflects a storied history: Expelled from Spain, and later forced to flee Algeria, their cookery was influenced by the nations they inhabited, as well as the trade routes that passed through these areas. Over the centuries, they collected recipes and flavors that came to form a unique and little-known culinary repertoire. The 85 recipes in this fascinating book are accompanied by a history of the Pied Noir and the story of the author's family. A glossary of culinary terms and menus for Pied Noir feasts are also included.

ISBN 0-7818-1082-5 · $24.95hc

The Art of Persian Cooking

Forough Hekmat

The nutritious, easy-to-follow recipes include such traditional Persian dishes as *Abgushte Adas* (Lentil Soup), *Mosamme Khoreshe* (Eggplant Stew), *Lamb Kabob, Cucumber Borani* (Special Cucumber Salad), *Sugar Halva,* and *Gol Moraba* (Flower Preserves).

From creating a holiday menu to determining which utensils to use, this insightful title covers a wide array of practical information to help even the novice chef prepare elaborate Persian dishes. The exotic fare is further enhanced by rich descriptions of the cultural and culinary history of Persian cuisine, without which it cannot be fully appreciated.

ISBN 0-7818-0241-5 · $12.95pb

Prices subject to change without prior notice. **To purchase Hippocrene Books** contact your local bookstore, visit www.hippocrenebooks.com, call (212) 685-4373, or write to: HIPPOCRENE BOOKS, 171 Madison Avenue, New York, NY 10016.